BLOOM
Founded by | arihant

Olympiad ACE

A Comprehensive Practice Book
for School Olympiads & Talent Search Exams

SCIENCE
Class 3

by
Rakhi Bisht

Olympiad ACE

BLOOM

Bloom Cap Edu Ventures Pvt. Ltd.

Administrative & Production Office

'Ramchhaya' 4577/15, Agarwal Road, Darya Ganj, New Delhi -110002
Tele: 011- 47630600, 43518550

PRICE: ₹125.00

PO No. : TXT-59-T063340-02-25

Published by Arihant Publications (I) Ltd.

For further information about the books log on to
www.bloomcap.org

Follow us on

Preface

"Future belongs to those Who prepares for it today"

School Olympiads are National & International level competitions conducted by different Government, Non-Government & Educational Organisations with the purpose of making the children ready to face competitive exams.

The challenging Questions asked in Olympiads motivate them to learn more & more and bring out the best result with improved academic performance. The Awards & Scholarship offered by Olympiads motivate children to aspire & strive for doing better and emerge out to be the best.

Science Olympiads

Being a Scientist or Engineer or Doctor has always been a dream of each school going child. A good command over Science is a must for any of these. Questions of Science Olympiads are structured to help students to develop scientific temperament & motivate them to understand the concepts of science. They also focuses on improving existing knowledge of a student by adding more information.

'Bloom Science Olympiad Study Book Class 3' is a perfect resource to Study & Practice for Olympiad Exams and other National & State Level Talent Search Exams & Other Competitions.

Some Special Features of Bloom Science Olympiad Study Books are;

- Chapterwise Exercises having different types of Objective Questions; Analytical, Applications, Remembering etc, at par with the Olympiad Level.
- Detailed Explanation for each question.
- Olympiad Pattern Practice Sets at the end.

This book is prepared by Expert Panel with the utmost care, still if you have any suggestions regarding its improvement then feel free to contact us at support@bloomcap.org. We will try to inculcate your suggestions in the further editions.

Contents

Chapter
01

Living and Non-living Things

We are surrounded by living things and non-living things.

- **Living things** can grow, move, breathe and reproduce.
  e.g. Plant, animal, human.
- **Non-living things** can be divided into two types :
  (i) Natural (occur in nature) e.g. Mountain, river, rain.
  (ii) Man-made (made by humans) e.g. Table, car, bench.

Characteristics of Living Things

1. Living things can grow.
2. They can move from place to place in search of food.
3. They need air to breath.
4. They need food and water to survive.
5. They give birth to young ones or reproduce.
6. They can feel the change in their surrounding.

- Non-living things do not breath, grow, feel, need food and reproduce.

Let's Practice

1. Pick the odd one out.

(a)  (b) 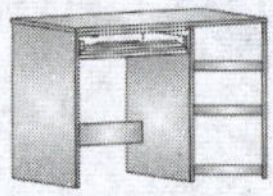 (c)  (d) 

2. Choose the non-living thing from the given picture below

(a)  (b)  (c)  (d) 

3. Man-made non-living things are
(a) balloon (b) chair (c) bottle (d) All of these

4. Which of the following is not made by natural thing?

(a)  (b)  (c)  (d) 

5. Living things need ...... and ...... to survive.
(a) air and shelter (b) food and water
(c) shelter and soil (d) food and shelter

6. If a living thing get food but no water and air, it will
(a) die (b) remain alive
(c) not grow (d) Both (b) and (c)

7. Living things take in ...... to breath.
(a) water (b) air
(c) food (d) None of these

8. Which of the following option is odd?
(a) Small girl - big girl (b) Small cat - big cat
(c) Small plant - big plant (d) Small rock - big rock

9. What are the three things needed by living things like animals from environment for their survival?
(a) Air, soil, water (b) Soil, water, food
(c) Soil, air, food (d) Air, water, food

10. The development of seed into plant shows which of the characteristic of living things?
(a) Movement
(b) Growth
(c) Reproduction
(d) Feel

11. All the process are common in all living things except
(a) breathing
(b) reproducing
(c) feeding
(d) walking

12. A sunflower always turns towards the Sun this shows that
(a) plants show movement
(b) plants are non-living things
(c) sunflower is a non-living thing
(d) plants do not grow

13. Pick the man-made non-living thing.
(a) Mountains
(b) Valleys
(c) Toys
(d) Rivers

14. Which of the following living organism can prepare their food by itself?

(a) Plant
(b) Dog
(c) Both can make
(d) No one can make

15. Match the following and choose the correct option.

	Column I		Column II
A.	We all need food	1.	Cannot move on its own
B.	A table in your room	2.	To prepare their food
C.	Plants needs sunlight, air and water	3.	To grow

Codes

	A	B	C
(a)	3	1	2
(b)	2	3	1
(c)	1	2	3
(d)	2	1	3

16. Choose the correct option.

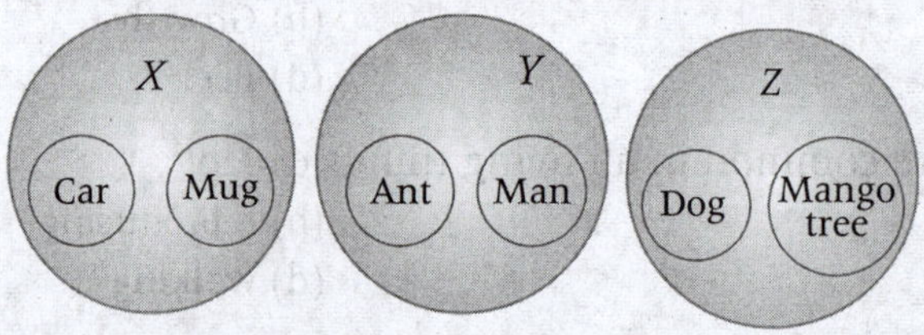

	X	Y	Z
(a)	Living	Living	Non-living
(b)	Living	Non-living	Living
(c)	Non-living	Living	Living
(d)	Non-living	Non-living	Living

17. Four students made statement about living and non-living thing.

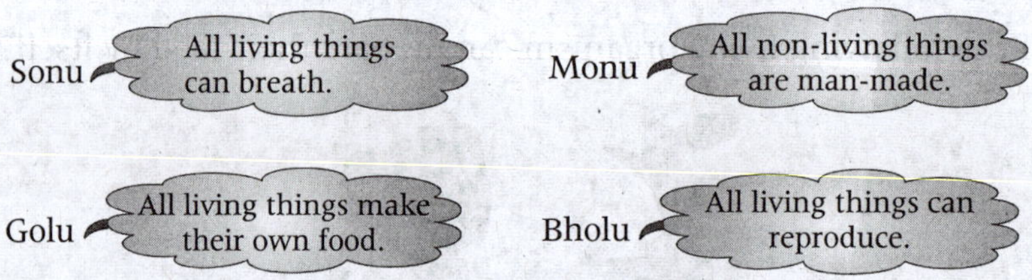

Choose which student(s) made an **incorrect** statement(s) ?

(a) Sonu and Monu
(b) Monu and Golu
(c) Golu and Bholu
(d) Only Monu

18. Which of the following is true?

(a) A stone can walk on its own
(b) Plants are non-living things
(c) Plants move from place to place
(d) All living things grow on their own

19. Is car a living thing?

(a) Yes, a car can move on its own
(b) No, car cannot reproduce
(c) Yes, car takes in petrol and gives out smoke
(d) Some cars are living things and some are non-living things

Chapter

02

Plants

- Plants are living things which can grow and make their own food.
- A plant has various parts namely roots, stems, leaves, flower, fruits, etc.

1. **Roots** This part of plant absorb water and minerals from soil and hold the plant firmly in the ground.

Plants	Consumable parts
Carrot, radish	Roots
Spinach, cabbage	Leaves
Cauliflower, broccoli	Flowers

Plants	Consumable parts
Apple, banana	Fruits
Rice, wheat	Seeds
Onion, garlic	Stems

2. **Stems** They support the plant and transport water and mineral from root to different part of plant.
3. **Leaves** This part of plant make food by the process of photosynthesis. Leaves of different plants have different shape and size.

Shapes of Leaves

Hand-shaped e.g. Maple | Heart-shaped e.g. Peepal | Oval-shaped e.g. Banyan | Round-shaped e.g. Lotus | Needle-like e.g. Spine

4. **Flower** They play an important role in reproduction and also turn into fruit in some plants.
5. **Seeds** New plants grow from seeds. They are usually protected inside the fruit. When the seed gets enough air, water and warmth, it grows into a baby plant.
6. **Fruits** They contains seed and these seeds are used to sown a new plant of same kind.

Let's Practice

1. In the along side figure of a plant, the function of part C is

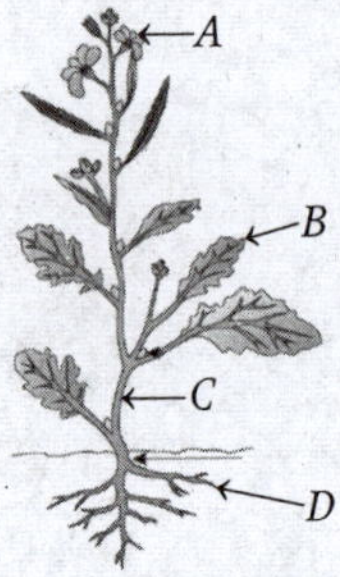

(a) helps in holding the soil together
(b) it get rid of excess water from the plant
(c) supplies food to all parts of the plant
(d) makes food for the plant

2. Part A shown in picture is the …… .

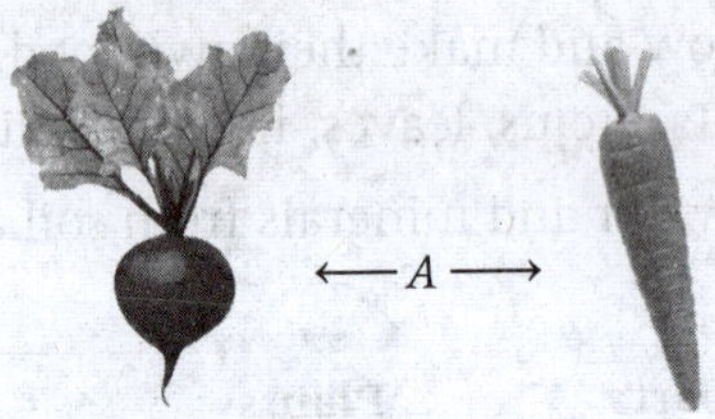

(a) stem (b) fruit (c) flower (d) root

3. Study the diagrams given below and answer the following question.

I.  II.  III. 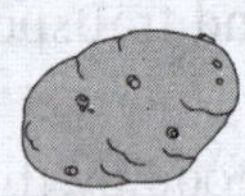 IV. 

Which of the above are stems?
(a) Only III (b) I and III (c) II and III (d) All of these

4. Which of these plants can be pulled out from the soil most easily?

(a)  (b)  (c)  (d) 

5. Out of the given plants / trees, which one bears fruits?

I.  II  III.  IV. 

(a) I and II (b) III and IV (c) II and III (d) Only III

6. When you are eating sugarcane, you are actually eating the

(a) fruit of sugarcane (b) stem of sugarcane
(c) roots of sugarcane (d) grains of sugarcane

7. Identify the correct relationship between the plant parts and choose the option which correctly signify '*A*'

 : Leaves : :  : *A*

(a) Root (b) Stems (c) Leaves (d) Flower

8. Mushrooms cannot make their own food because ....

I. they grow in the shade. II. they are white in colour.
III. they do not have green leaves. IV. they do not need food to grow.

(a) Only III (b) I and II (c) Only II (d) All of these

9. Match the following columns.

	Column I		Column II
A.	Leaves	1.	Protect seeds
B.	Roots	2.	Produce fruits
C.	Flowers	3.	Absorb mineral
D.	Fruits	4.	Food factory

Codes

	A	B	C	D		A	B	C	D
(a)	4	3	2	1	(b)	3	4	2	1
(c)	4	2	1	3	(d)	4	3	1	2

10. Match the statements in List-I with the correct picture in List-II.

List-I	List-II	List-I	List-II
A. It fixes the plant in the soil.	1.  Tap root (main root)	C. It make food for the plant.	3. 
B. It takes water from the roots to the leaf.	2. 	D. It changes into fruit.	4. 
		E. It grows into a new tree	5. 

Codes

	A	B	C	D	E		A	B	C	D	E
(a)	4	2	1	5	3	(b)	2	4	1	5	3
(c)	1	4	2	3	5	(d)	4	1	2	3	5

11. Match the following with their names.

Column I	Column II
A. Shrubs	1. Money plant
B. Herbs	2. Grapevine
C. Climbers	3. Rose
D. Creepers	4. Grass

Codes

	A	B	C	D		A	B	C	D
(a)	3	4	2	1	(b)	3	4	1	2
(c)	4	3	2	1	(d)	4	2	1	3

12. State the following statement as True (T) or False (F).

I. Plants are non-living things.
II. Climbers do not need support to stand.
III. Money plant is a big plant.
IV. Some plants are big.
V. Most leaves are green in colour.

Choose the correct option.

	I	II	III	IV	V		I	II	III	IV	V
(a)	F	F	F	T	T	(b)	F	T	F	F	T
(c)	F	F	T	T	F	(d)	T	F	T	T	F

13. Fill in the right words in the empty boxes.

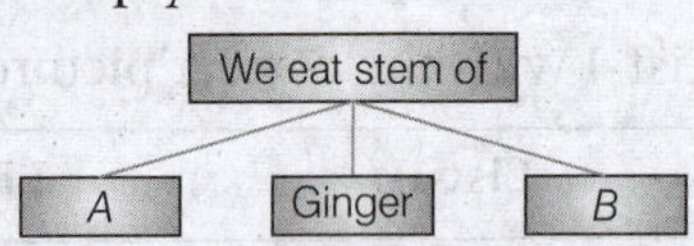

(a) *A* - Turnip and *B* - Carrot
(b) *A* - Sugarcane and *B* - Radish
(c) *A* - Sugarcane and *B* - Potato
(d) *A* - Potato and *B* - Cabbage

14. Four friends went to see a garden and made a statement each about the leaves of a plant.

Which friend was wrong?

(a) Akriti, Komal and Arjun (b) Akriti only (c) Komal and Rakhi (d) Arjun and Rakhi

15. Sonal put a potted plant near her window as shown in figure.

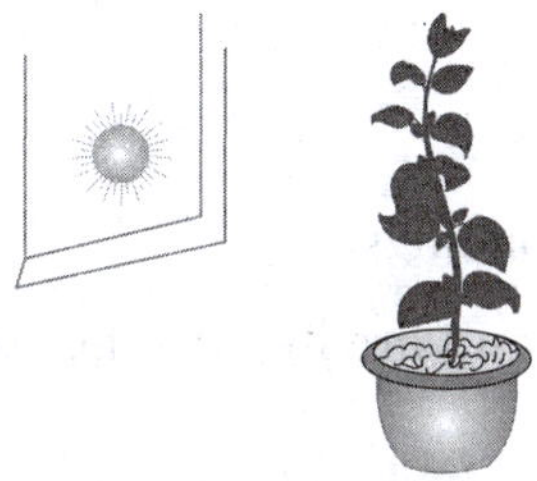

However, within a week, Sonal's plant died. Why did this happen?

I. She forgot to water the plant.

II. She closed the window on a rainy day and the plant died.

III. The plant died during the night when there was no sunlight.

(a) Only I (b) I and III (c) I, II and III (d) None of these

16. The diagram given below shows a rose plant.

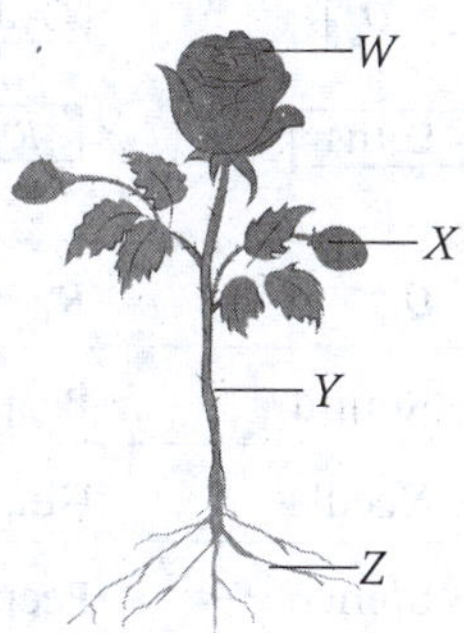

Which one of the parts shown above W, X, Y and Z support the leaves and carries the food made by the leaves to the rest of the plant?

(a) *W* (b) *X* (c) *Y* (d) *Z*

17. Elliot took four identical plants *A, B, C* and *D* and removed a different part from each plant as shown in the table given below.

Plants	Parts that were removed
A	All flowers
B	All leaves
C	All fruits
D	All root

Which plant will eventually die?

(a) Plant *A* (b) Plants *B* and *D*

(c) Plants *A* and *C* (d) Plant *D*

18. The function of the stem in *Cactus* plant is to ......
(a) protect the plant
(b) make and store food
(c) store food
(d) absorb water from the surroundings

19. The leaves of *Cactus* are small and are like needles so that ....
(a) they can make food faster
(b) they can reduce water loss to the atmosphere
(c) they can receive more sunlight
(d) they can exchange more gases with the surroundings

20. Study the given flow chart carefully and identify P, Q, R and S.

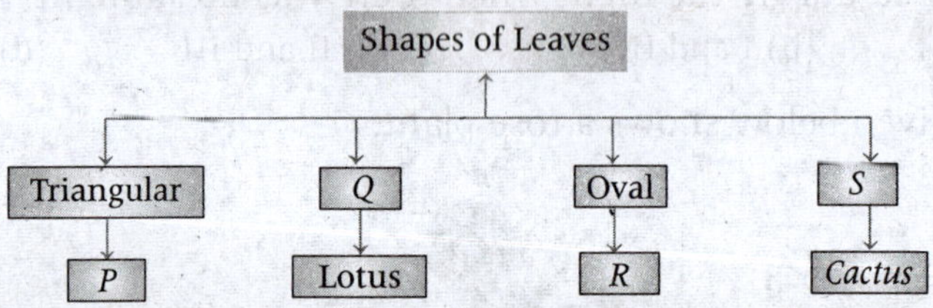

	P	Q	R	S
(a)	Guava	Round	Peepal	Spine
(b)	Pine	Needle	Guava	Spine
(c)	Guava	Spine	Peepal	Needle
(d)	Peepal	Round	Guava	Spine

Chapter

03

Animals

Animals based on their Habitat

Terrestrial animals that live on land. e.g. Dog, cat, camel, etc.

Aquatic animals that live in water throughout their life. e.g. Fishes.

Aerial animals that can fly, their forelimbs are modified into wings, e.g. Birds.

Animals based on their Behaviour

Pet animals that people keep in their houses, they do not harm humans. e.g. Dog, cat, rabbit, etc.

Domestic animals which are useful for humans, people keep them in farm, they provide milk, egg etc., to human. e.g. Cow, hen, goat, etc.

Wild animals which live in jungle and are dangerous for human as they can harm them. e.g. Lion, tiger, etc.

Farm animals that are reared for a purpose that is for their meat, milk, hair of something else, e.g. Sheep, goat, cow, buffaloes, etc.

Animals based on their Feeding Habits

Herbivorous animals which eat only plants. e.g. Goat, cow, deer, etc.

Carnivorous animals which eat only animal flesh. e.g. Lion, wolf, etc.

Omnivorous animals which eat both plants and flesh of other animals. e.g. Bear, crow, etc.

Animals based on their Eating Habits

Types of animals and their method of eating habits	Examples
Those animals that first stored their food in stomach and then chew it, are known as cud chewing animals?	Cow, buffaloes, sheep, etc.
Those animals that have two long pairs of incisors that are used like chisels to grow on hard food like nuts and wood are called rodents or grazing animals.	Rat, rabbit, squirrels, etc.
Those animals that shallow their food as it is, are called swallowing animals.	Snake, frog, lizards, etc.
Those animals that tear the flesh of other animals using their sharp pointed teeth are called flesh tearing animals.	Tiger, lion, foxes, etc.
Those animals that have long thin tube which help them to suck nectar or blood from other organisms are called sucking animals.	Bees, butterflies, mosquitoes, etc.
Those animals that use their tongue to lap up water or milk are called lapping animals.	Dogs, cats, etc.

Let's Practice

1. Which of the following is/are terrestrial animals?

(P)	(Q)	(R)	(S)	(T)

Choose the correct option.

(a) P and Q (b) Q, R, S (c) Q and T (d) Q and S

2. Which of the following animals feed on both plants and animals?

(I)	(II)	(III)	(IV)

(a) I and II (b) II and IV (c) III and IV (d) I, II and IV

3. Match the animals with their food.

Animal	**Food**
A.  Elephant	1.  Mouse
B.  Horse	2.  Carrot
C.  Cat	3.  Sugarcane
D.  Rabbit	4.  Grass

	A	B	C	D		A	B	C	D
(a)	4	3	1	2	(b)	3	4	2	1
(c)	3	4	1	2	(d)	3	4	2	1

4. Which of the following is not correctly paired?

(a) Rabbit - Gnaw (b) Cow - Chew (c) Tiger - Tear (d) Frog - Lap

5. Match the following columns.

	Column I		Column II
1.	Pet animals	P.	Cat
2.	Domestic animals	Q.	Cow
		R.	Goat
		S.	Dog
		T.	Sheep

Codes

	1	2		1	2
(a)	P, Q,	S R, T	(b)	R, T	P, Q, S
(c)	P, S	Q, R, T	(d)	Q, R, T	P, S

6. On the basis of feeding habits animals are classified into different groups. Fill the blank with correct option.

	X	*Y*	*Z*
(a)	Herbivorous	Carnivorous	Omnivorous
(b)	Carnivorous	Herbivorous	Omnivorous
(c)	Carnivorous	Omnivorous	Herbivorous
(d)	Omnivorous	Carnivorous	Herbivorous

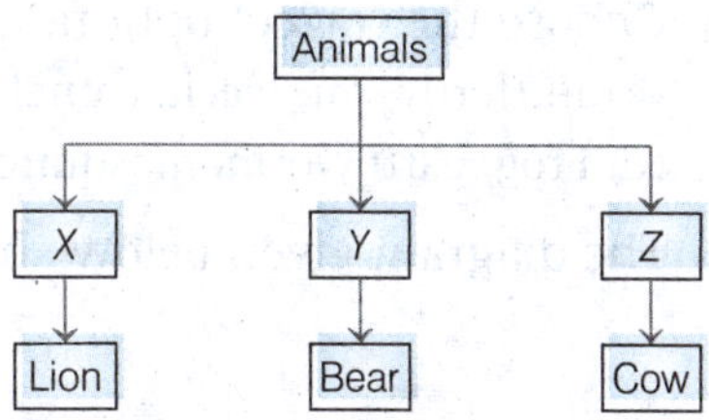

7. Which one of the following statement(s) is/are incorrect w.r.t. fish and Jaguar?

(a) One breathe through gills, while the other breathe through lungs
(b) One has fur, while the other has scales
(c) One has wings, while the other has limbs
(d) One lay eggs, while the other gives birth to its young alive

8. Study the classification diagram shown below.

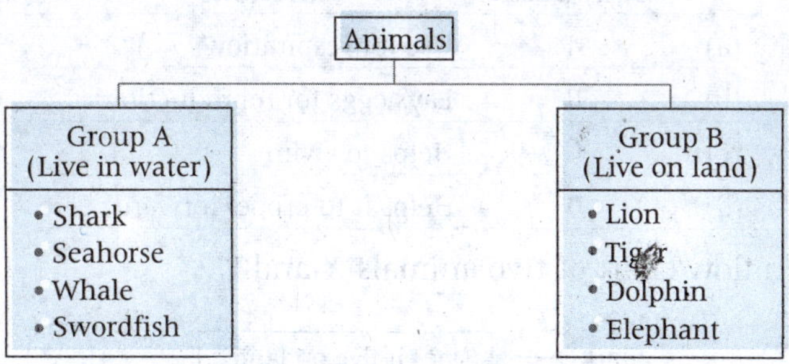

Which animal in the group is incorrectly placed?

(a) Shark (b) Dolphin (c) Lion (d) Elephant

9. Write true or false for the following statements.

I. Cow, buffalo, camel and horse are cud-chewing animals.
II. Kangaroo, zebra and deer are omnivores.
III. Food keeps animal sick and weak.
IV. A mosquito has a long tube to suck blood.

Codes

	I	II	III	IV		I	II	III	IV
(a)	T	F	F	T	(b)	T	T	F	F
(c)	F	T	F	T	(d)	F	F	T	T

10. A home for fish is known as
(a) a formicarium (b) a vivarium (c) an aquarium (d) None of these

11. Read the clues and write the names of these animals ....

I. It has a long sticky tongue ....
II. It swallow soil ....
III. It sucks blood ....
IV. It carries load for us ....

Choose the correct option.
(a) Butterfly, rat, leech, camel
(b) Snake, rabbit, mosquito, horse
(c) Frog, earthworm, mosquito, donkey
(d) Butterfly, earthworm, leech, camel

12. The diagram given below shows a fish and *A*, *B*, *C* and *D* are its body parts.

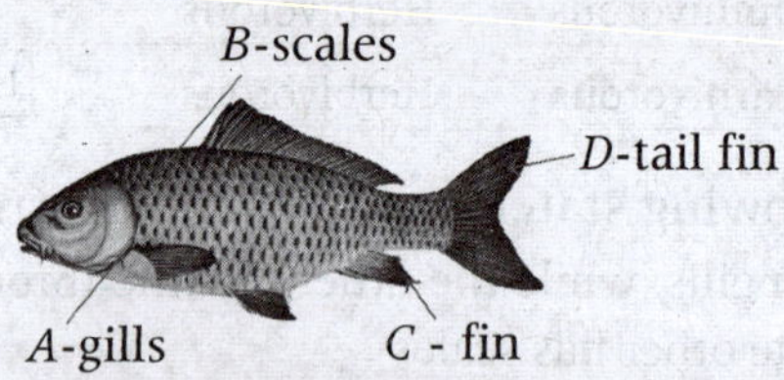

The following table relates the mentioned body parts to their functions. Which one of the following is incorrect?

	Body parts	Functions
(a)	*A*	Use for respiration
(b)	*B*	Lays eggs for reproduction
(c)	*C*	Helps to swim
(d)	*D*	Helps it to propel forward

13. Study the given flow chart of two animals *X* and *Y*

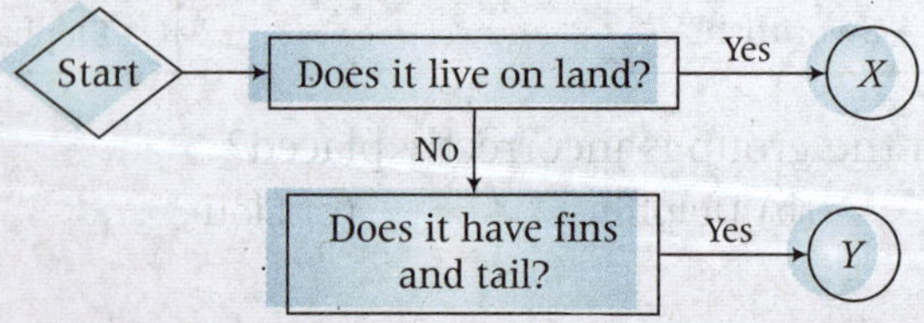

Which of the following best represents *X* and *Y* respectively?

	X	*Y*		*X*	*Y*
(a)	Giraffe	Dolphin	(b)	Bear	Shark
(c)	Tiger	Cat	(d)	Dolphin	Zebra

14. Unscramble the letters given in the box to get the name of an animal. Now select the correct option regarding this animal

U	T	R	L	B	E	Y	F	T

(a) It sucks nectar
(b) It carries load for us
(c) It has a long sticky tongue
(d) It swallow soil

15. Read the passage and choose the correct options.
......(*A*) .... animals are those that live on the land. They have ...... (*B*) ...... to walk and have well-developed ...... (*C*) .... organs. Their claws and ...... (*D*) .... are very sharp which enables them to catch and eat their prey.

	A	*B*	*C*	*D*
(a)	Amphibian	legs	sense	nails
(b)	Amphibian	limbs	sense	teeth
(c)	Terrestrial	legs	sense	teeth
(d)	Terrestrial	hands	sense	mouth

16. Complete the given food chain.
Grass, Grasshopper, ______, Snake, Eagle.

(a) 
Lion

(b) 
Cat

(c) 
Dear

(d) 
Frog

Chapter 04

Birds

- Birds are flying animals. They have feathers and wings to fly.
- Body of birds is different from rest of animals as they have beak instead of mouth, claws instead of feet, streamlined body, hollow bones and wings instead of hands.

Beaks of Birds

- Strong, **curved beak** used to break hard nuts, e.g. Parrot, parakeets, etc.
- Strong, short and hard beak used to break nuts and grain. Sparrow, peacock, etc.
- Strong, sharp and hooked beak used to tear flesh, e.g. Eagle, vulture, etc.
- **Chisel**-shaped beak used to make holes in tree, e.g. Woodpecker, hooper, etc.
- **Broad and flat beak** with holes used to find insects in muddy water, e.g. Duck, goose, etc.
- Long and pointed beak used to suck nector and catch fishes, e.g. Sunbird and kingfisher.

Claws of Birds

- **Slender claws**, three toes on front and one on back used to hold the branch of tree. e.g. Sparrow, crow, etc.
- Two **toes** pointing upward and two pointing downward used to climb on tree. e.g. Parrot, woodpecker, etc.
- Sharp and strong **talons** used to catch their prey, e.g. Eagle, vulture, etc.
- **Webbed foot** used to swim in water, e.g. Duck, crane, etc.

Nesting Habits

Birds make their nest to lay eggs. The material used by birds to make their nest are as follows

- Penguins pebbels and stones.
- Vulture, Eagles tall trees in shallow cup-shaped.
- Tailor bird large leaves, cotton and hair.
- Ducks holes in ground and covered them with grasses.
- Koels do not make their nest they lay egg in crow's nest.

Flightless Birds

These birds cannot fly. They rely on their ability to run or swim.
e.g. Kiwi, penguins, ostrich, etc.

Let's Practice

1. Which bird use its beak like straw?

(a) Sunbird (b) Tailor bird
(c) Hooper (d) Woodpecker

2. Chisel-shaped beak is used to ....

(a) catch the prey (b) break nut and grain
(c) find insect (d) make holes in tree

3. Which of the following bird have three toes on front and one on back?

(a) Crow (b) Parrot
(c) Hen (d) Sparrow

4. Which bird has the largest egg in the world?

(a) Emu (b) Ostrich
(c) Vulture (d) Eagle

5. Identify the bird whose claws / feet is given and function of feet / claw.

(a) Parrot - climb on tree
(b) Crow - hold the branch
(c) Parrot - hold the branch
(d) Crow - catch the prey

6. Nest of which bird is shown in the figure given below.

(a) Tailor bird (b) Vulture
(c) Weaver bird (d) Duck

7. Which of the following bird can fly?

(a) Emu (b) Humming bird
(c) Penguin (d) Turkey

8. The bird shown in picture belong to which group of bird?

(a) Perching bird
(b) Scratching bird
(c) Flesh eating bird
(d) Climbing bird

9. Match the column, and identify the type of beak birds have

A.  Eagle	1. Broad and flat
B.  Goose	2. Curved beak
C.  Parrot	3. Chisel-shaped
D.  Hoopoe	4. Strong and hooked

Codes

	A	B	C	D
(a)	2	1	4	3
(b)	2	3	4	1
(c)	4	1	2	3
(d)	4	3	2	1

10. Write down the information about the birds in the table given below

Name of birds	Colour of birds	Types of beak
Parrot	*A*	Curved
Duck	White	*B*

Choose the correct option.

	A	*B*
(a)	Green	Pointed
(b)	Green	Flat
(c)	Yellow	Flat
(d)	Yellow	Pointed

11. Choose the correct statement about birds nest.

(a) The penguins makes a nest on the ground with the pebbles and stones
(b) The weaver bird uses its beak like a needle to make their nest
(c) A sparrow makes its nest in the shallow cup shape
(d) Vulture pecks at a tree to make their nest

12. Which of the following is the main difference between an owl and a bat?

Owl Bat

(a) Owls have feathers and beak but bats do not
(b) Bats have ears, owls do not
(c) Owls fly in the day, bats in the night
(d) Bats feed on flowers, while owls eat insects

13. Identify the correct relation

Woodpecker : Wood :: Sunbird : ———— .

(a) Fish (b) Nectar
(c) Grain (d) Flesh

14. Its cold and icy where we live. So we have to huddle in tight. We have wings but we cannot fly, so we cannot soar to a great height.
Guess who am I?

(a) Sparrow (b) Peacock
(c) Parrot (d) Penguin

15. Read the following passage very carefully.

An animals has flown into the classroom. The students are very excited and decide to name it Para-Para. It has a large dark beak but the feathers are very colourful. The students feed it with some ripe fruits.

Identify to which group Para-Para is related

(a) Mammal (b) Insect
(c) Fish (d) Bird

16. Four students made a statement each about the bird shown below.

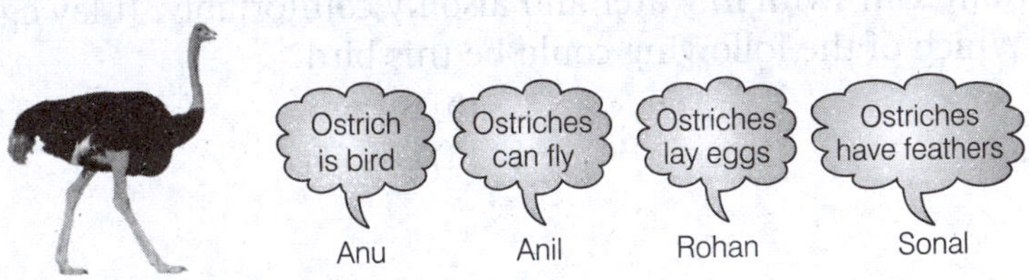

Which student did not make a correct statement?

(a) Anu (b) Anil
(c) Rohan (d) Sonal

17. In the given Venn diagram out of *P, Q, R* and *T* which describe the tailor bird correctly.

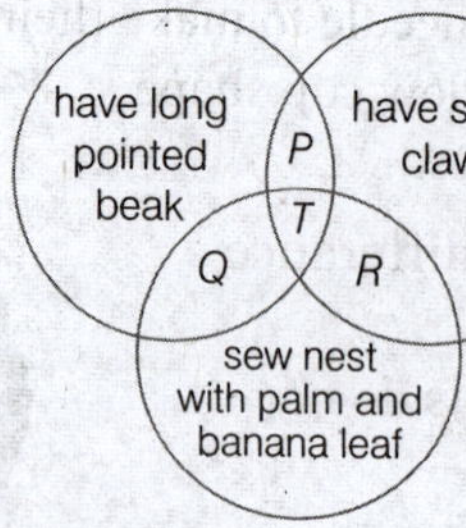

Choose the correct option.

(a) *P* (b) *Q* (c) *R* (d) *T*

18. Study the given flow chart and identify *A*, *B* and *C*.

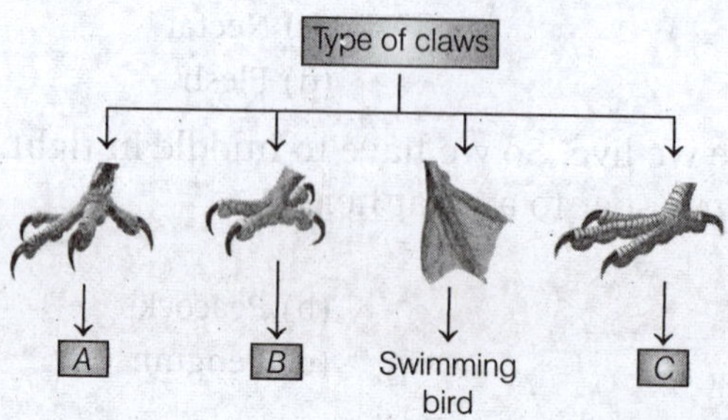

	A	*B*	*C*
a.	Perching bird	Climbing bird	Flesh eating bird
b.	Flesh eating bird	Perching bird	Scratching bird
c.	Flesh eating bird	Climbing bird	Scratching bird
d.	Climbing bird	Scratching bird	Perching bird

19. A particular bird can swim in water and also fly comfortably. It lay eggs to reproduce. Which of the following could be this bird?

(a) Owl (b) Swan

(c) Parrot (d) Ostrich

Chapter 05

Human Body

- Human body consist of organs, which forms organ system.
- There are five sense organ in human body which help us to understand our surroundings, i.e. eyes (to see), ears (to hear), nose (to smell), tongue (to taste) and skin (to feel). They are also called external organs. Skin is the largest sense organ of the body.
- Internal organs are the part of our body which we cannot see directly. They are :

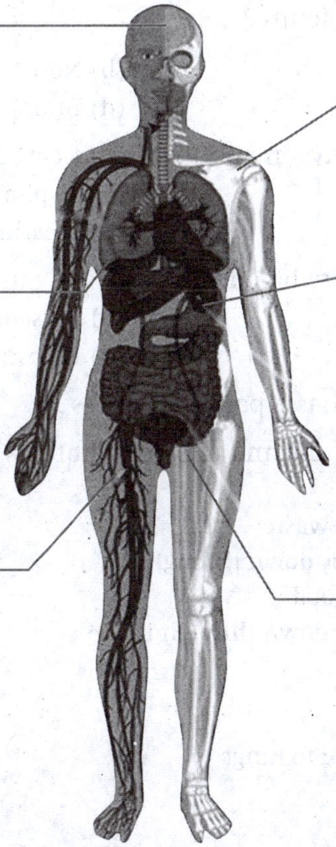

Nervous System
The nervous system is to control and coordinate the working of other systems. It is made up of the brain, spinal cord and nerves.

Skeleton System
The skeletal system is made up of bones and joints. It provides support to our body and allows us to move.

Respiratory System
The respiratory system helps us to intake air and use oxygen from it. The organs of this system are the nose, larynx, windpipe and lungs.

Excretory System
The excretory system helps us to throw out wastes from the body.

Circulatory System
The circulatory system helps us to carry things from one part to the other parts of the body. The parts of this system are the heart, artery, veins and blood.

Digestive System
The digestive system helps us to digest the food, we eat. The organs of this system are the mouth, food pipe, stomach, intestine and rectum.

Organ System of the Human Body

Let's Practice

1. The organ in the diagram helps us in

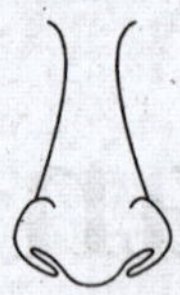

(a) seeing (b) smelling (c) hearing (d) dealing

2. The heart rate of a healthy person is ...... per minute.

(a) 70 (b) 78 (c) 72 (d) 73

3. Our sense of ...... and ...... tells us that food is hot and tasty.

(a) touch and hearing
(b) touch and taste
(c) smell and sight
(d) sight and taste

4. Which one of the following organ is protected by the bone shown in given picture?

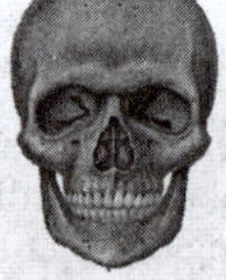

(a) Ears
(b) Nose
(c) Eyes
(d) Brain

5. The process of taking in oxygen and giving out carbon dioxide is called

(a) digestion
(b) respiration
(c) circulation
(d) breathing

6. Which system helps to carry blood to all parts of our body?

(a) Respiratory system
(b) Muscular system
(c) Circulatory system
(d) Digestive system

7. The diagram given below has a part labelled as *X*

Identify the diagram carefully and answer what is *X* and its function?

(a) Blood vessels - to remove waste
(b) Foodpipe - the food moves down through it
(c) Blood vessels - to carry blood
(d) Windpipe - the air moves down through it

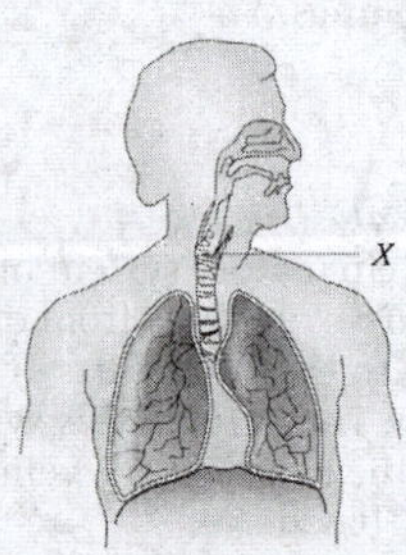

8. The function of heart is ....

(a) to transfer oxygen to lungs
(b) to transfer carbon dioxide to lungs
(c) to pump blood
(d) to pump nutrients

9. Consider the following two statements

I. There are 206 bones in our body.

II. Two or more bones are connected together to form joint.

Choose the correct option.

(a) Both I and II are correct
(b) Both I and II are incorrect
(c) Only I is correct
(d) Only II is correct

10. Select the correct sequence of the organ of respiratory system through air will pass after inhalation.

(a) Nose → Lungs → Windpipe → All parts of body
(b) Lung → Windpipe → Nose → All parts of body
(c) Nose → Windpipe → Lungs → All parts of body
(d) Lung → Nose → Windpipe → All parts of body

11. Using the clue, unscramble the letters and find the organ system.

(A) "Controls all action of our body"

E	V	O	N	R	S	U

(a) Skeleton
(b) Muscular
(c) Nervous
(d) Digestive

12. Identify the correct relation and find *X* and *Y*

Digestive system : *X* :: Skeleton system : *Y*

	X	*Y*		*X*	*Y*
(a)	Food pipe	Brain	(b)	Stomach	Bone
(c)	Kidney	Bone	(d)	Brain	Liver

13. Which of the following organs send message to the brain?

(a) Heart
(b) Lungs
(c) Skin
(d) Nerves

14. Match the following columns.

Column I	Column II
A. Kidneys	1. Digestive system
B. Carbon dioxide	2. Nervous system
C. Nerves	3. Excretory system
D. Food pipe	4. Respiratory system

Codes

	A	B	C	D		A	B	C	D
(a)	2	3	1	4	(b)	3	4	2	1
(c)	3	2	1	4	(d)	4	3	2	1

15. Rohan was playing with his friends, suddenly he fell down and broke his ribcage. Which of his organs are now in danger?

I. Small intestine II. Large intestine III. Heart IV. Lungs

Choose the correct option.

(a) I and II (b) II and III (c) II and IV (d) III and IV

16. Consider the following functions.

Movement, Running, Support, Protection, Shape,

These functions are part of which system?

(a) Muscular system (b) Nervous system
(c) Circulatory system (d) Skeletal system

17. Refer to Venn diagram, identify what is *P*?

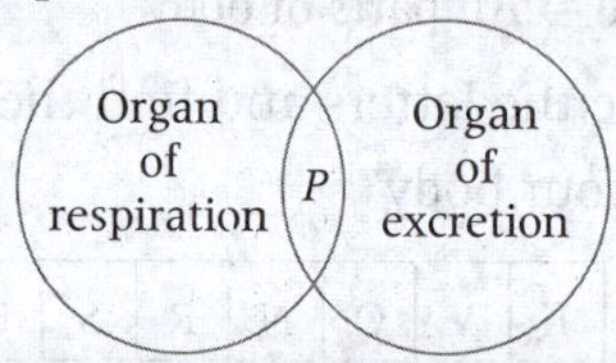

Choose the correct option.

(a) Kidney (b) Skin
(c) Lungs (d) Both (a) and (c)

18. Select the option that correctly identifies *X*, *Y* and *Z*.

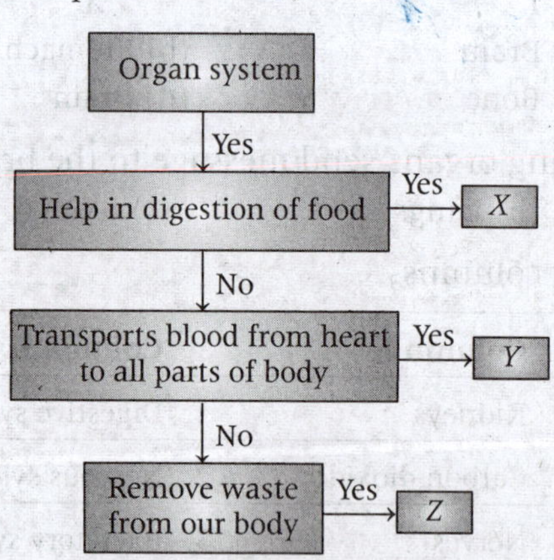

	X	*Y*	*Z*
(a)	Respiratory system	Digestive system	Circulatory system
(b)	Circulatory system	Digestive system	Excretory system
(c)	Digestive system	Circulatory system	Excretory system
(d)	Digestive system	Respiratory system	Circulatory system

Chapter 06

Food

Food is essential for all living beings. Plants and animals are the major sources of food.

Nutrients in Our Food

Balance diet contain accurate amount of all the nutrients in it.

Types of Food

Energy giving food	Body building food	Protective food
Provide us energy to do work. carbohydrates and fats are known as energy giving food. Fats provide more energy than carbohydrates.	Helps us to grow. They helps in maintaining our bones and muscles strong.	They help our body to fight against disease. Vitamins and minerals prevent us from falling sick.
e.g. Potatoes, bread, sugar, rice (carbohydrates) and oil, butter, ghee (fats).	e.g. Pulses, milk, meat, egg, etc. are rich in protein.	e.g. Fruits and vegetables.

We must include water and roughage in our diet.

- **Water** It helps to maintain our body temperature. We must drink at least 6-8 glasses of water everyday.
- **Roughage** It is important for the proper digestion of food. Raw vegetables and fruits are rich source of roughage.

Healthy Cooking and Eating Habits

- Uncooked foods are known as raw foods.
- The food gets soft and tasty when we cook. It is easily digested.
- Rice and pulses are examples of cooked food whereas fruits and milk are examples of raw food.
- Avoid junk food and uncovered food sold by hawkers.
- Always wash your hands and mouth before and after every meal.
- Chew your food well and eat slowly.
- Wash vegetables and fruits before cutting and cooking.

Let's Practice

1. Which of the following is an animal product?

(a) 

(b) 

(c) 

(d) 

2. Idli and dosa are mostly eaten by people living in

(a) Punjab (b) Gujarat (c) Assam (d) Tamil Nadu

3. We get pulses, vegetables and nuts from.........

(a) plants (b) animals (c) Both (a) and (b) (d) None of these

4. Identify the relation one is done for you Carbohydrate : Rice :: Protein : ...... :: Ghee : ....

Choose the correct option.

(a) Fruits, Vitamin (b) Pulses, Carbohydrate

(c) Junk food, Fats (d) Meat, Fats

5. The food item prepared from cow's milk is

I. 

II. 

III. 

IV. 

Choose the correct option.

(a) I and III (b) Only II (c) II and III (d) I, II and IV

6. Look at this picture and answer the question given below

The above food items are examples of

(a) healthy food (b) nutritious food (c) junk food (d) None of these

7. The given food items are sources of

Vegetable oil, Sunflower oil, Cotton seed, Soybean

(a) Carbohydrates (b) Proteins (c) Minerals (d) Fats

8. Select the correct option regarding the given food items.

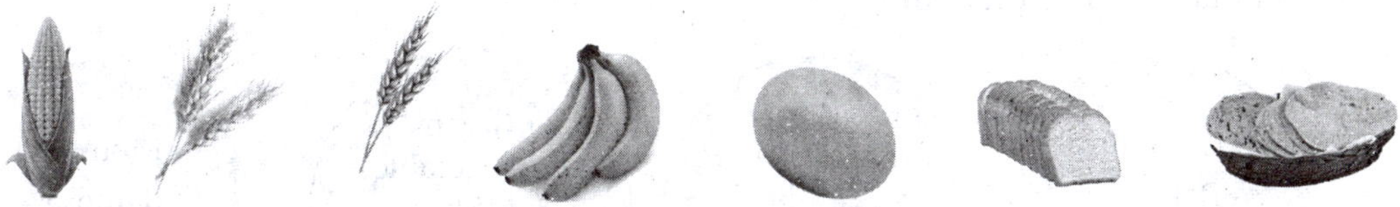

Corn Wheat Rice Banana Potato Bread Chapatis

(a) These food items are sources of proteins
(b) These food items are sources of carbohydrates
(c) These food items does not provide us energy
(d) These food items are protective foods

9. Growing children should eat which type of food?
(a) Energy giving
(b) Body building
(c) Both (a) and (b)
(d) Only (a)

10. Mineral essential for the formation of teeth and bone is ....
(a) protein
(b) iron
(c) calcium
(d) copper

11. When we are fasting, from where do our body get energy ?
(a) Carbohydrates
(b) Proteins
(c) Stored fats
(d) Water

12. Which of the following is not a healthy eating habit?
(a) Talking and laughing while eating
(b) Chewing food properly
(c) Eating food after washing hand
(d) All of the above

13. Select the correct option regarding the given fruits and vegetables.

Orange, Lemon, Cabbage, Potato, Lime, Carrot, Onion

I. Fruits and vegetables keep the eyes, bones and teeth healthy.
II. They also protect us from illness.
III. They gives us lots of energy when we are hungry.
IV. These food lacks nutrient value.

Choose the correct option.
(a) II and III
(b) Only IV
(c) I and II
(d) I and III

14. Given below are plates of students of class 3, which plate shows the right amount of nutrients (balance diet) in it.

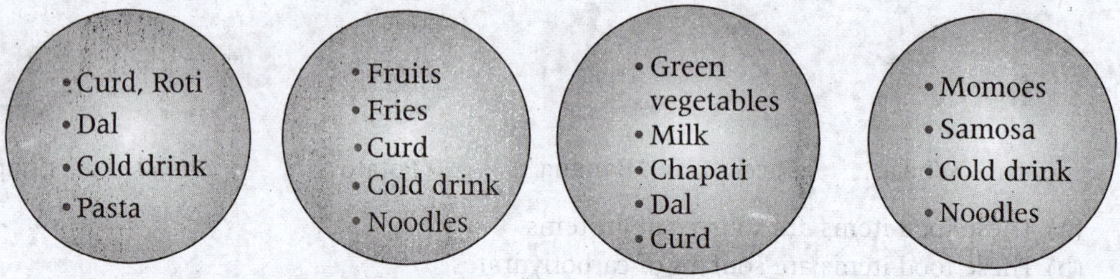

I II III IV

Choose the correct option.

(a) Student I and II
(b) Student III and IV
(c) Student III only
(d) Student IV only

15. Read the given statements.

I. Some food items can be eaten raw without cooking like apple, banana, oranges, etc.

II. Most of the food items need to be cooked before they can be eaten.

III. Cooking makes the food tasty, healthy and digestible.

Which of these statement(s) is/are correct?

(a) I and II
(b) III and IV
(c) I, II and III
(d) Only III

16. Solve the riddle

I am used a lot in Indian cooking,
I am an antiseptic also,
I am yellow in colour,
Who am I ?

(a) Chilli
(b) Turmeric
(c) Pepper
(d) Cardamom

Chapter 07

Housing, Clothing and Occupation

Housing

- We need a house to live in, our house protects us from heat, cold, storm and rain. It also protect us from animals and thieves.
- The types of houses we build depend upon our needs.

1. **Permanent House** These houses cannot be shifted from one place to another.
   - **A kachcha house** is made up of mud and straw and found mostly in villages. It is not very strong, e.g. Hut.
   - **A pakka house** is made up of bricks, iron, wood, glass, concreate, etc., and mostly found in towns. It is very strong, e.g. Apartment, bungalow, multistorey buildings, etc.
2. **Temporary House** Some people live at a place for a short time, so they make houses with wood, mud, etc., so that they can be easily moved from one place to another. Such kind of houses are called temporary house like tent, caravan, houseboat, stilt house, igloo, etc.

A Good House

It should have the following features :

1. Well-ventilated
2. Door and window should have proper wire-netting.
3. Proper drainage system
4. Have open spaces and plants.
5. Cleaned toilets and bathrooms
6. Dustbins having lids.
7. Everything should be kept at its proper place.

Clothing

- Clothes are one of our basic needs.
- We wear clothes to cover our body and to protect us from the heat, cold and rain.
- Clothes are made up of fibres which can be obtained from natural or man-made sources. Clothing in India varies according to weather, occasions, region, culture, profession, etc.

Summer season

Clothes made from cotton

Winter season

Woolen clothes made from wool

Rainy season

Waterproof clothes made from PVC

Occupation

The work people do to earn money is called their occupation. Different people have different occupations.

	Occupation		Work
1.	Doctor	a.	Treats patients
2.	Chemist	b.	Gives medicines prescribed by a doctor
3.	Engineer	c.	Designs and construct roads, building, etc.
4.	Mechanic	d.	Repairs machines and vehicles
5.	Teacher	e.	Teachers students in schools and colleges
6.	Postman	f.	Brings letters and parcels
7.	Policeman	g.	Maintain law and order
8.	Carpenter	h.	Makes and repairs wooden things and furnitures
9.	Tailor	i.	Stitches our clothes
10.	Pilot	j.	Flies an airplane
11.	Actor	k.	Performs in plays or movies
12.	Barber	l.	Cut our hair
13.	Cobbler	m.	Repairs our footwear
14.	Architect	n.	Designs buildings and houses
15.	Plumber	o.	Repair leaking taps or pipelines
16.	Mason	p.	Makes houses
17.	Green grocers	q.	Sells fruits and vegetables

Let's Practice

1. Among the given option choose a kachcha house
   (a) hut (b) bungalow (c) multistorey (d) skyscraper
2. Which house is made on wooden poles?
   (a) Igloo house (b) Stilt house (c) Houseboat (d) Caravan
3. Bricks are used to build houses because they are
   (a) hard and strong (b) made of wood (c) made of plants (d) free from germs
4. Cotton fibre is obtained from
   (a) sheep (b) goat (c) plant (d) worm
5. Paheli wants to present her friend a gift made from wool. Which of the following is made up of wool?
   (a) Bag (b) T-shirt (c) Saree (d) Shawl
6. Campers, soldiers and construction workers use this type of house. This type of house is called
   (a) A caravan (b) A hut (c) A houseboat (d) A tent house
7. The following description is about the special type of house.
   These houses are found in cold countries. They have round or dome-shaped roofs. Usually eskimos live in these type of house. This type of house is called
   (a) stilt (b) caravan (c) houseboat (d) igloo
8. Match the following columns.

	Column I		Column II
A.	A hut	1.	Snow
B.	An igloo	2.	Mud and water
C.	A houseboat	3.	Canvas
D.	A tent house	4.	Wooden

Codes

	A	B	C	D		A	B	C	D
(a)	2	1	4	3	(b)	1	2	3	4
(c)	1	2	4	3	(d)	4	2	3	1

9. The house as shown in the diagram is built in a place where?
   (a) Climatic conditions are very cold
   (b) Winds blows very fast
   (c) It rains heavily
   (d) None of the above

10. Material used in an umbrella is
(a) wool (b) cotton (c) waterproof (d) None of these

11. Igloo : Ice :: Caravan : ?
(a) Water (b) Tent (c) Wheels (d) Villa

12. Which type of clothes we wear in month of December?

(a)  (b)  (c)  (d) 

13. A/An .... can be made using the materials shown here.

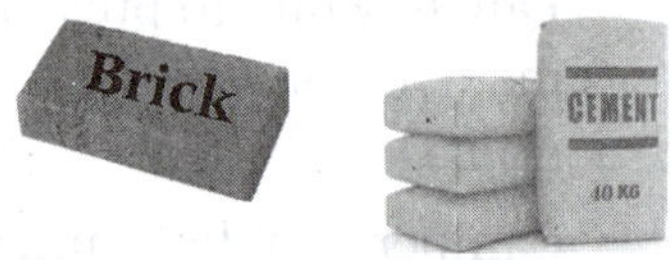

(a) Houseboat (b) Igloo
(c) Caravan (d) Pakka house

14. Which house is used by the people who keep moving from one place to another ?

(c)  (d)  (c)  (d) 

15. Divya has gone to Antartica on a vacation with her family. Select the option which she can wear over there
(a) Shorts (b) Skirt (c) Sweater (d) Raincoat

16. Refer to the given picture and answer the question

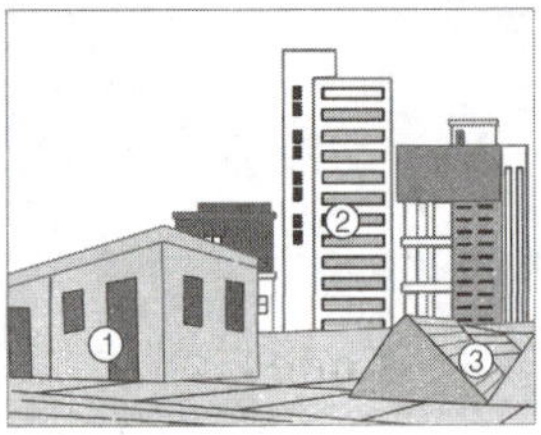

The given house 1 and 2 are
(a) Portable and temporary house
(b) Temporary and permanent house
(c) Permanent and temporary house
(d) Permanent house only

17. Match the following columns.

	Column I		Column II
A.	Sunlight	1.	To let the smoke go out.
B.	Chimneys	2.	To sit and enjoy the fresh air and warmth of sunlight.
C.	Verandah	3.	Keeps mosquitoes and flies away.
D.	Wire netting	4.	Keeps the rooms free from germs.

Codes

	A	B	C	D		A	B	C	D
(a)	1	2	3	4	(b)	4	3	2	1
(c)	4	1	2	3	(d)	3	4	2	1

18. Select the correct match.

	Tools	Professional
(a)		Policeman
(b)	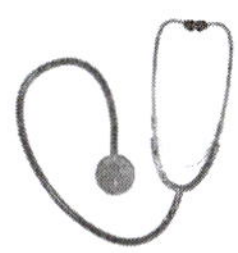	Doctor
(c)		Barber
(d)		Farmer

19. Refer the given conversation among three friends who are going to a school.

Nitin - There was a theft in our house, my mother is going to call a '*P*'

Supriya - My fathers motorbike has broken down, he is going to call a '*Q*'

Gagan - My grandmother is suffering from a toothache, my father is taking her to a '*R*'.

Select the correct option regarded *P*, *Q* and *R*

	P	*Q*	*R*
(a)	Greengrocer	Barber	Farmer
(b)	Tailor	Doctor	Carpenter
(c)	Policeman	Mechanic	Doctor
(d)	Plumber	Teacher	Cobbler

Chapter 08

Water and Weather

- About 71% of our Earth is covered with water in the form of ice (solid), water (liquid) and vapour (gas).
- There are two main sources of water, natural sources (rainwater, river, lake, etc.) and man-made sources (dams, well, tubewells, etc.).
- Apart from these sources some water (rain water) sweep into ground and stored in the form of **underground water**.

Water Cycle

It shows continuous movement of water with in the Earth and atmosphere. This involves following processes

- **Evaporation** water convert into vapour form.
- **Condensation** water vapour convert into liquid droplets and make clouds.
- **Precipitation** water droplets join together and form clouds, when the clouds become heavy from water droplets they fall down as rain.
- **Water Cycle** Collection the rainwater fills the river, lake, pond, etc., and this cycle repeat again and again. Hence, its called water cycle.

Weather

- It is the daily state of the wind, sun-shine, clouds of a place at a particular time.
- Weather can be sunny, rainy, windy, etc., it may change everyday. When Sun heats the Earth, warm air goes up, the cool air rushes to takes its place. So the wind blows.
- Gentle winds are called **breeze**, very fast winds are called **gale** and wind with great speed and rains is called **storm**.
- When same type of weather remains for longer period of time, it is known as **season**.
- Season divided into 5 types namely **Summer** (hot), **rainy** (humid), **winter** (cold), **autumn** (fall of leaves) and **spring** (flowers bloom).

Let's Practice

1. What is the natural source of pure water?
   (a) Ponds (b) Rain (c) Sea (d) Oceans
2. The process of converting of water into vapour is called ....
   (a) condensation (b) boiling (c) evaporation (d) heating
3. Arrange the following processes in correct sequence according to the water cycle.
   (a) Evaporation, Precipitation, Collection, Condensation.
   (b) Condensation, Evaporation, Precipitation, Collection.
   (c) Collection, Precipitation, Condensation, Evaporation.
   (d) Evaporation, Condensation, Precipitation, Collection.
4. The condition of air surrounding us with respect to temperature, wind and rain at a particular place or time is called ....
   (a) season (b) climate (c) weather (d) humidity
5. Wet clothes dry faster on
   (a) humid day (b) sunny day
   (c) windy day (d) Both (b) and (c)
6. Which of the following affects the weather?
   I. The Sun affects the weather.
   II. The wind affects the weather.
   III. The clouds and the rain affects the weather.

   Choose the correct option.
   (a) Only I (b) Only III (c) I and II (d) I, II and III
7. Arrange the five seasons of India in the correct chronological order.
   (a) Rainy, Summer, Winter, Autumn, Spring (b) Spring, Summer, Autumn, Winter, Rainy
   (c) Autumn, Winter, Spring, Rainy, Summer (d) Summer, Rainy, Autumn, Winter, Spring
8. During summer, we need to drink plenty of water as we lose a lot of it while ......
   (a) excreting (b) sweating
   (c) cooling (d) heating
9. In a season, weather is pleasant. It is a season of flowers and butterflies, the trees have new green leaves. Identify the season.
   (a) Summer (b) Autumn
   (c) Rainy (d) Spring
10. The clothes in summer dry faster than in winters because of ....
    (a) high evaporation (b) low evaporation
    (c) high condensation (d) low condensation

11. State the following statement as True (T) or False (F).

I. Lack of rain over a long period of time result in drought.

II. Too much rain causes flood.

Choose the correct option.

	I	II		I	II		I	II		I	II
(a)	T	F	(b)	F	T	(c)	T	T	(d)	F	F

12. Ice $\xrightarrow{X}$ water $\xrightarrow{Y}$ water vapours

Complete the given flow chart and choose the correct option for *X* and *Y*.

	X	*Y*
(a)	Heating	Cooling
(b)	Cooling	Heating
(c)	Melting	Evaporation
(d)	Evaporation	Condensation

13. Read the following statements carefully.

I. Weather may be windy, sunny, cloudy or rainy.

II. Weather does not change from place to place.

III. Weather changes only during the day.

Choose the incorrect option.

(a) I and II
(b) II and III
(c) Only II
(d) I and III

14. I am the coldest time of the year. Travel, sports and outings become difficult in my period. Cold dry air blows in my times. Tell me who I am?

(a) Summer season
(b) Rainy season
(c) Autumn
(d) Winter season

15. The Sun heats up the water present in seas, rivers, lakes and ponds.

The water gets heated up and changes into water vapour.

The water vapour present in air is called ... (*A*) ... It is highest in the ... (*B*) ... season.

(a) *A*-Fog, *B*-Winter
(b) *A*-Misty, *B*-Winter
(c) *A*-Fog, *B*-Rainy
(d) *A*-Humidity, *B*-Rainy

Chapter
09

Matter and Materials

Matter

- Anything that has mass and occupies space is defined as **matter**.
- Everything around us air, water, rocks even we are made of matter.
- Matter exists in three forms of states : Solid, liquid and gas.

Solid	Liquid	Gas
Has its own shape	Takes the shape of its containers	No shape of its own
Has volume	Has volume	No fixed volume
Can't compress	Can't compress	Can be compressed

Changes in States of Matter

- Solid converts to liquid on melting.
- Liquid converts to gas on evaporation.
- Gas converts to liquid on condensation (i.e. water vapour to water).
- Liquid converts to solid on freezing.

$$\text{Solid} \underset{\text{Freezing}}{\overset{\text{Melting}}{\rightleftharpoons}} \text{Liquid} \underset{\text{Condensation}}{\overset{\text{Evaporation}}{\rightleftharpoons}} \text{Gas}$$

Materials

- The matter from which useful things can be made of is called a **material**, e.g. Wood, steel, glass, etc.
- Materials have different properties like, opaque, transparent, stretching, rough, smooth, waterproof, conduct heat and electricity, etc.

	Material	Properties	Uses
1.	Glass	Hard, waterproof, transparent.	Aquarium, window pane.
2.	Plastic	Light,waterproof, strong, durable.	Raincoat, plastic bags.
3.	Wood	Light, strong, poor conductor of heat of electricity.	Door, handle of pot, furniture.
4.	Metal	Hard, strong, durable, good conductor of heat and electricity.	Iron nail, kettle, pots, machines.
5.	Paper	Light, flexible.	Kite, envelopes, books
6.	Rubber	Flexible, waterproof.	Toy, tyre.

Let's Practice

1. As steam is related to gas then chair is related to
   (a) solid
   (b) gas
   (c) liquid
   (d) None of these
2. Find the odd one out.
   (a) Table
   (b) Pencil
   (c) Milk
   (d) Wood
3. In the given figure, solid converts into liquid, this process known as

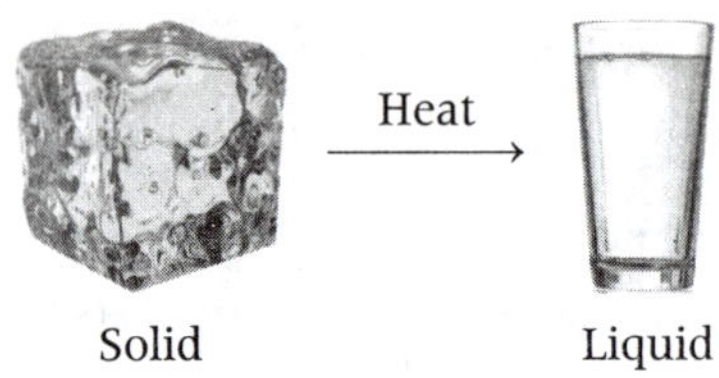

   (a) melting
   (b) condensation
   (c) evaporation
   (d) freezing
4. Which of these can be found in all 3 states of matter?
   (a) Wax
   (b) Kerosene
   (c) Wood
   (d) Water
5.

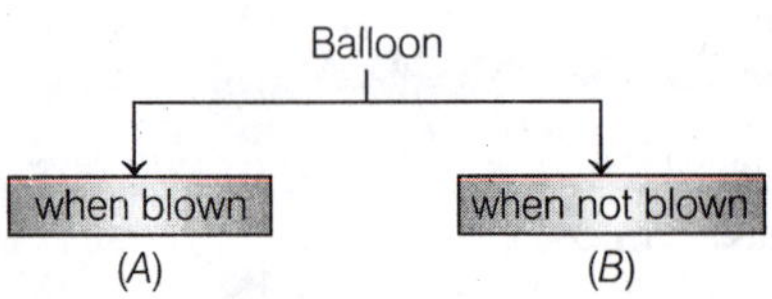

   Based on the given diagram, choose the correct option.
   (a) *A* is heavier than *B*
   (b) *B* is heavier than *A*
   (c) Both are have equal weight
   (d) None of these
6. From the following list, count the solids and liquids by selecting the correct option.
   Eraser, water, juice, oil, paper, book, oxygen, carbon dioxide, chair, coffee, laptop, air, smog.
   (a) Solids (4) Liquids (4)
   (b) Solids (5) Liquids (4)
   (c) Solids (5) Liquids (3)
   (d) Solids (3) Liquids (4)
7. It has a volume that stays the same, but it can change shape. What is it?
   (a) Gas
   (b) Solid
   (c) Mass
   (d) Liquid

8. Look at each object and match it to the material it is made from.

A.		1.	Tree
B.		2.	Metal
C.		3.	Rubber
D.		4.	Glass

Codes

	A	B	C	D		A	B	C	D
(a)	2	1	4	3	(b)	3	2	4	1
(c)	2	4	1	3	(d)	4	3	1	2

9. We can smell a perfume in the nearby room because
(a) perfume are very loose and flow easily
(b) it has been sprayed in the nearby room
(c) your nose is too sensitive
(d) None of the above

10. Select the incorrect matching.

(a) 
Water (Liquid)

(b) 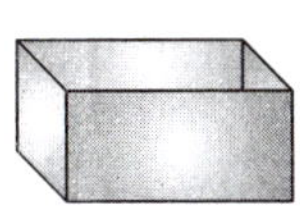
Box (Solid)

(c) 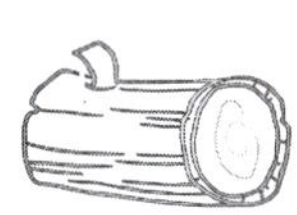
Wood (Solid)

(d) 
Vapour (Liquid)

11. What will happen, if water spilled on the surface of a plastic table is left untouched for sometime?
(a) The water will change into ice
(b) The amount of water will become more
(c) The amount of water will become less
(d) Both (a) and (c)

12. Refer to the alongside given diagram and select the correct option regarding it.

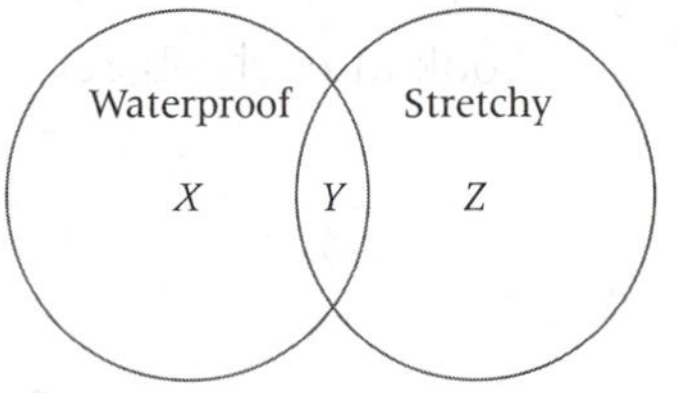

(a) X-Rubber, Y-Glass (b) Z-Umbrella, X-Plastic
(c) X-Wood, Y-Plastic (d) X-Umbrella, Z-Rubber

13. Complete the given flow chart.

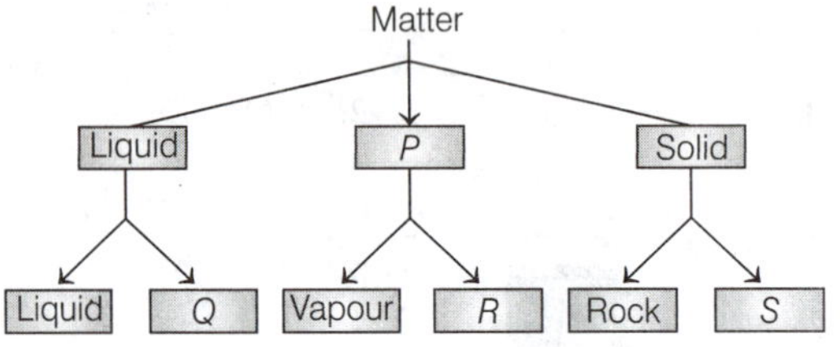

	P	Q	R	S
(a)	Gas	Milk	Carbon dioxide	Clock
(b)	Book	Gas	Hammer	Juice
(c)	Liquid	Oxygen	Clock	Paper
(d)	Solid	Chair	Computer	Pepsi

14. Which pattern is being followed in the following series :

Brick : milk : carbon dioxide : : Bone : lotion : water vapour

(a) Liquid : solid : gas (b) Gas : solid : liquid (c) Solid : liquid : gas (d) Solid : gas : liquid

15. Piyush and Komal were standing as shown here. Piyush waved to Komal and she smiled in reply. Sheet X can be made up of

(a) wood (b) iron
(c) plastic (d) glass

16. Anshika wanted to find material X. She put the material over a container and poured some water onto it as shown in figure given below. She found that no water was collected in the container. What material could X be ?

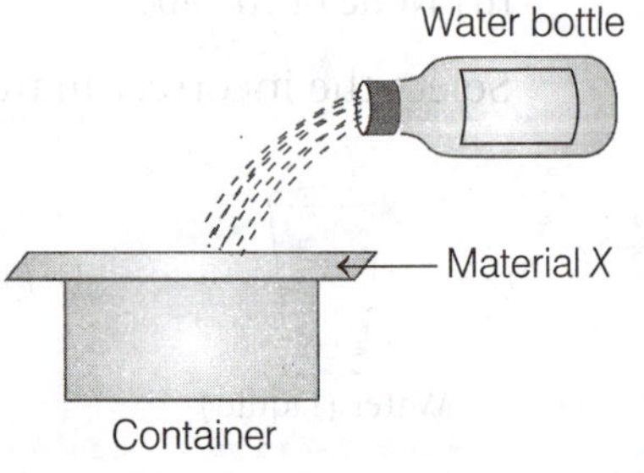

(a) Cloth (b) Glass
(c) Paper (d) Cardboard

Chapter

10

Measurements

- **Length** is measured in metre and centimetre. The standard unit of length is metre (m). Length is measured using a ruler, meter rod or measuring tape.

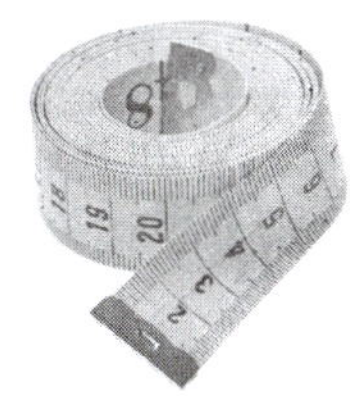

$$1 \text{ kilometre} = 1000 \text{ metre}$$
$$1 \text{ metre} = 100 \text{ centimetre}$$

- **Mass** is measured in kilogram and gram. The standard unit of mass is kilogram (kg). It is measured using a weighing scale or electronic balance.

$$1 \text{ kilogram} = 1000 \text{ gram}$$
$$1 \text{ gram} = 1000 \text{ milligram}$$

- **Volume** is measured in millilitre, litre, cubic metre (m^3) and cubic centimetre (cm^3). The standard unit for measuring volume is litre (L). Volume can be measured using measuring cylinder or a measuring glass.

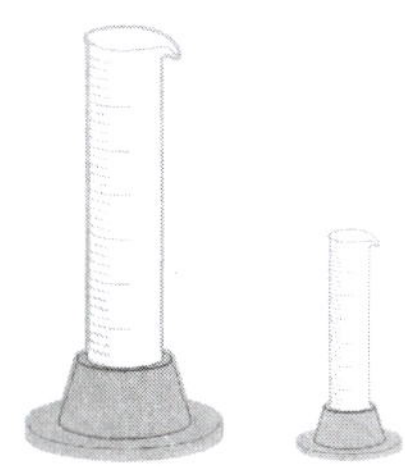

$$1 \text{ litre} = 1000 \text{ millilitre},$$
$$1 \text{ cubic metre} = 10^6 \text{ cubic centimetre}$$

- **Time** is measured in hours, minutes and seconds. The standard unit for measuring time is **second** (s). Time can be measured using a watch or a clock.

$$1 \text{ hour} = 60 \text{ minutes}$$
$$1 \text{ minute} = 60 \text{ seconds}$$

- **Temperature** is measured in degree celsius (°C) or degree fahrenheit (°F). The temperature refers to the hotness or coldness of a body.
- **Thermometer** is used to measure it. The body temperature of a normal person is 37°C or 98.6°F.

Let's Practice

1. Which of these can be measured with a ruler (scale)?
   (a) Eggs (b) Milk (c) Cloth (d) Sugar

2. Which of these is needed to measure the weight of a rock?
   (a) A thermometer (b) A watch (c) A balance (d) A metric ruler

3. The amount of liquid (a container can hold) is called
   (a) capacity (b) time (c) length (d) temperature

4. Which of the following tools is used for finding the temperature at which water boils?

(a) 

(b) 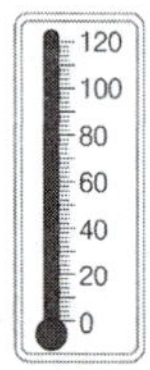

(c) 

(b) 

5. Which of the following things can be measured easily?
   I. Milk in a bottle II. Sugar in a bowl III. Width of hair IV. Air around you
   (a) Only I (b) Both I and III (c) Only II (d) Both I and II

6. Write the correct units for measuring the following objects.

(I) 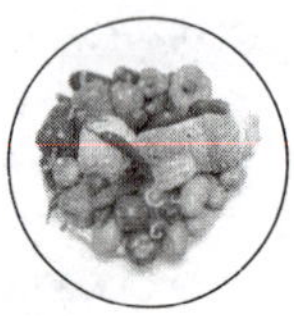

(II) 

(III) 

(IV) 

Choose the correct option.

	I	II	III	IV
(a)	cm	L	m	s
(b)	g	L	cm	s
(c)	kg	mL	m	s
(d)	kg	mL	cm	s

7. Match the following columns.

	Column I		Column II
A.	Length of a room	1.	°C
B.	Volume of milk	2.	metre
C.	Mass of a book	3.	measuring can
D.	Temperature on a cold day	4.	kilogram

Codes

	A	B	C	D		A	B	C	D
(a)	2	3	1	4	(b)	4	3	2	1
(c)	2	4	3	1	(d)	2	3	4	1

8. Which measuring instrument would you prefer to measure the length of following items?

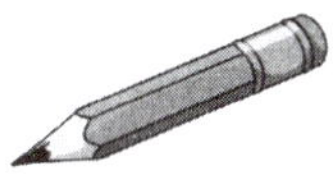
(I)

(II)

(III)

(a) Electronic balance
(b) Meter rod
(c) Ruler
(d) Measuring cylinder

9. Which of the following statement is incorrect?
(a) Small amounts of liquids like shampoo and eye drops are measured in millilitre.
(b) Standard unit for measuring mass is kilogram.
(c) Standard unit for measuring length is centimetre.
(d) Standard unit for measuring time is second.

10. Ritu wants to purchase 2m cloth for her uniform. Which of the following measuring instrument will shopkeeper use to measure 2m cloth?

(a) 
(b) 
(c) 
(d) 

11. I. The smaller the container, the lesser will be its capacity to hold liquids.
II. Temperature is the measure of how cold or hot an object.
Which of the following statement(s) is/are correct?
(a) Statement I is true, II is false.
(b) Statement II is true, I is false.
(c) Both I and II are true.
(d) Both I and II are false.

12. Salman want to find out the distance from his school to home. In which unit of measurement does he gets the distance?
(a) kl
(b) km
(c) kg
(d) h

13. Rhea completed her homework in 1 hr while Ritika took 40 min to complete the same homework. Who took less time?
(a) Rhea
(b) Ritika
(c) Both complete the home at work same time
(d) Can't say

14. The table below shows the number of steps taken by 5 children to measure the width of a room.

Name	No. of Steps
Ajay	9
Salman	10
Sameer	8
Adnan	7
Shivani	11

Who has the shortest step?

(a) Ajay (b) Salman (c) Adnan (d) Shivani

15. Sara has 60 m of ribbon. If she cuts 20 m ribbon from it, then what length of ribbon will be left?

(a) 60 m (b) 40 m (c) 20 m (d) 30 m

16. What is the weight of the books in kilograms?

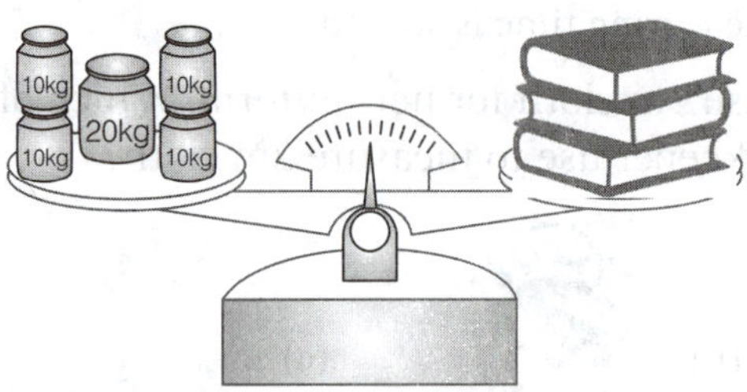

(a) 60 kg (b) 50 kg (c) 40 kg (d) 30 kg

17. Complete the given flow chart and choose the correct option for A, B and C.

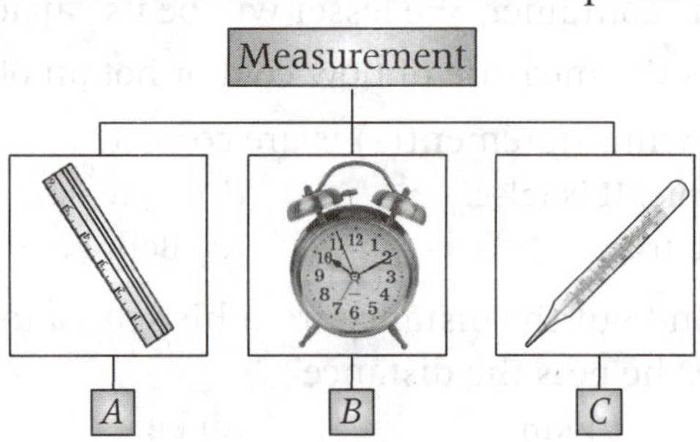

	A	B	C
(a)	Metre (m)	Celsius (°C)	Second (s)
(b)	Metre (m)	Second (s)	Celsius (°C)
(c)	Second (s)	Metre (m)	Celsius (°C)
(d)	Celsius (°C)	Metre (m)	Second (s)

Chapter
11

Motion and Transport

Motion

- When a body is continuously changing its position with respect to the surroundings, then we say that the body is in motion.
- Movement of an object from one place to another is called motion. Motion take place whenever force is applied. When a boy throw a ball, movement of the ball takes place due to the force exerted by the boy.

  Motion is classified into two types :

  1. **Uniform Motion** When a body travels equal distance in equal interval of time. e.g. Movement of Moon around the Earth.
  2. **Non-uniform Motion** When a body travels unequal distance in equal interval of time. e.g. Car moving on a bumpy road.
- Uniform motion is further divided into various types

Uniform Motion

Linear/Rectilinear motion
Motion in a straight line.
e.g. March past of soldiers

Periodic motion
Motion that repeats itself after same period of time.
e.g. Pendulum clock

Circular motion
Motion where objects move along a circular path.
e.g. Hands of a clock

Transport

- A system or means of conveying people or goods from one place to another is called transport.
- The vehicles we use to travel from one place to another are known as means of transport, e.g. Car, train, aeroplane, ship, etc.
- Means of transport are categorised as

Means of Transport

Land transport
The vehicles that move on land. e.g. Bus, train, etc.

Water transport
The vehicles that move in water. e.g. Ships, boat, etc.

Air transport
The vehicles that move in air.
e.g. Aeroplanes, rocket, etc.

- Ambulance, fire engine, police van and postal van are some special means of transport.

Let's Practice

1. A girl is covering equal distance in equal interval of time. What type of motion is she having?
   (a) Linear motion (b) Periodic motion (c) Circular motion (d) Uniform motion

2. Which of these shows circular motion?
   (a)  (b) 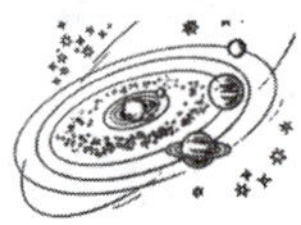 (c)  (d) 

3. Which of the following means of transportation is the cheapest?
   (a) Air transport (b) Road transport (c) Water transport (d) None of these

4. From the following, write the fastest and slowest means of transportation.

I

II

III

IV

V

VI

   Fastest and slowest means of transportation are
   (a) I and II (b) V and III (c) VI and III (d) VI and II

5. Name any two slow means of transport run by animals
   (a) horse, bullock cart (b) rickshaw, tonga
   (c) donkey, tonga (d) bullock cart, tonga

6. Which of the following is used by soldiers to travel under water?
   (a) Sailboat (b) Ship (c) Submarine (d) Boat

7. The wheels were used in making the transport vehicles. Name four such vehicles
   (a) tonga, horse, donkey, camel (b) ox, scooter, camel, tonga
   (c) bullock cart, tonga, camel cart, cycle (d) cycle, motorcycle, camel, horse

8. X and Y are mean of water transport.

	X	*Y*
(a)	Scooter	Boat
(b)	Submarine	Car
(c)	Ship	Motor boat
(d)	Jet scooter	Jetplane

9. Which of these animals were used for travelling from place to place?
   I. Horses II. Monkey III. Camels IV. Dogs
   (a) Only I (b) Both I and III (c) Both III and IV (d) I, II and III

10. Select the odd one out on the basis of mode of transport.

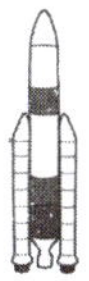
(a)

(b)

(c)

(d)

11. Consider the following flow chart and choose the correct option.

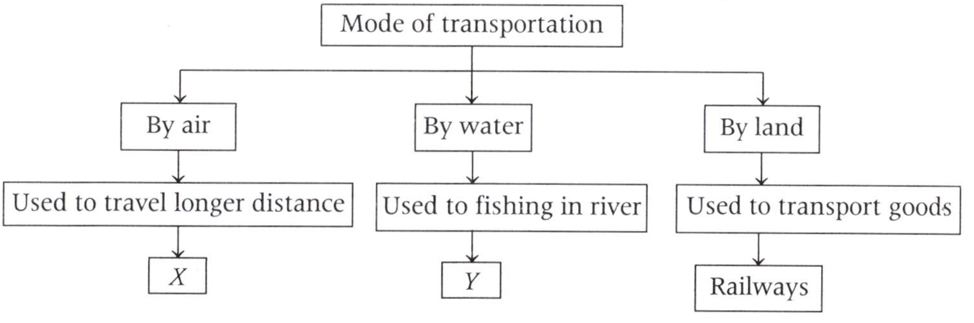

	X	Y		X	Y
(a)	Aeroplane	Submarine	(b)	Jetpack	Boat
(c)	Aeroplane	Boat	(d)	Boat	Spacecraft

12. Choose the incorrectly matched.

(a) Air transport → fastest mode of transportation.

(b) Water transport → cheapest mode of transportation.

(c) Land transport → expensive mode of transportation.

(d) Space transport → can only be used in space.

13. Rohan wants to travel from one country to another. Which of the following mode of transportation should be avoided, if Rohan is in hurry?

(a) Land transport (b) Air transport (c) Water transport (d) All of these

14. Find the odd one out.

(a) A moving car's wheel (b) A rotating ceiling fan

(c) A bouncing ball (d) Moving of a car around a circular pathway

15. Which means of transport among the following is environment friendly?

(a) Bus (b) Scooter (c) Bicycle (d) Car

16. In which of the following groups, the odd one out is encircled incorrectly?

(a) Train, Bus, (Cycle), Car (b) Helicopter, Jet plane, Spacecraft, (Car)

(c) (Train), Helicopter, Spacecraft, Jet plane (d) Bus, Car, (Ship), Scooter

17. Which of the following is used to transport huge amount of cargo?

(a) Railways (b) Ships (c) Aeroplanes (d) Bicycles

Chapter 12

Our Environment

Air

- Every empty space is filled with a mixture of gases, called air. Gases present in air are **Nitrogen, Oxygen, Carbon dioxide** and many more.
- Air also contains **water vapour, dust particles, germs, smoke** and **harmful gases**.

Soil

- Soil is the top most and loose layer of **Earth** that covers the surface of our planet.
- The soil includes disintegrated rocks, humus, air, water, etc.
- Rocks when break into their constituent parts by the action of Sun, wind and rain, leads to formation of soil. It takes thousands of years for the formation of soil.
- The dead part of plants and animals called **humus**.
- Soil is classified into various types :

Sandy soil	Clayey soil	Loamy soil
• It contains sand particle in it. • It does not hold much water. • Plants do not grow well in it.	• It contains clay particles. • It can hold a lot of water, but does not drain well. • It is used by potters.	• It is a mixture of sandy and clayey soil. • It is the best for the growth of the plants.

Pollution

Any changes in the environment which result in its harmful effect is called pollution. Different types of pollution are

Air pollution	Water pollution	Soil pollution	Noise pollution
• Air pollution is the introduction of harmful material into the atmosphere. • It is caused by the release of harmful chemicals, smoke by vehicles, factories, etc.	• Water pollution is the contamination of water bodies. • It is caused by release of toxic material, hot water or steam into water bodies by factories, leakage of sewage pipes, littering of wrappers and plastic bottles in water.	• Soil pollution is the contamination of soil with harmful substance. • It is caused due to use of harmful chemicals in crop field, littering of waste here and there.	• Noise pollution is amount of noise in the surrounding that disrupts the natural balance. • It is caused due to excess use of loud-speakers, mikes, horns by people. It affects the mental health of a person.

Let's Practice

1. Rain and wind can break rocks into small pieces. What happens to these small pieces when they break away?
   (a) Plants use them for energy
   (b) They turn into earthworms
   (c) They become food for animals
   (d) They become part of the soil

2. Which of the following things should we do to keep our environment clean?
   I. Throw garbage only at collection points.
   II. Stop using plastic bags.
   III. Water should be conserved.
   Choose the correct option.
   (a) I and II (b) II and III (c) I and III (d) I, II and III

3. Match the Column I with Column II and select the correct option.

Column I	Column II
A. Noise that pollution	1. Bathing in rivers with soap
B. Air that pollution	2. Use of plastics
C. Water pollution	3. Factory chimneys
D. Soil pollution	4. Unnecessary blowing horns

Codes

	A	B	C	D		A	B	C	D
(a)	4	3	1	2	(b)	1	2	3	4
(c)	4	3	2	1	(d)	3	4	1	2

4. Humus, silt, clay and sand are all parts of
   (a) soil (b) plants (c) animals (d) rocks

5. Which of the following children made an incorrect statement about the activities you should do to save water and make air fresh

Jay: Do not burn dry leaves and bushes

Sonal: Burn fire crackers

Jitu: Wash floor daily with clean drinking water

Anu: Plant more trees

(a) Jay and Jitu (b) Jitu and Sonal (c) Anu and Jay (d) Jitu and Anu

6. Match the following columns.

	Column I		Column II
A.	Soil that cannot hold water.	1.	Clayey soil
B.	Soil that is good for plant growth.	2.	Sandy soil
C.	Soil particles are very fine.	3.	Loamy soil

Codes

	A	B	C		A	B	C
(a)	1	2	3	(b)	2	3	1
(c)	3	2	1	(d)	1	3	2

7. The overuse of plastic articles is not good for us and the environment. We should take steps to minimise their use. What can we do to minimise overuse of plastics?

I. We should use paper bags.

II. We should give away old plastic toys to others who can use them.

III. We should throw the plastic container.

Choose the correct option.

(a) Only I (b) Only II (c) I and II (d) I and III

8.

I am invisible,
I am essential for existence of life,
When I move then my name is change

Who am I ?

(a) Water (b) Air (c) Rock (d) Coal

9. Identify the true statement from the following

(a) Sandy soil is best for the growth of plants.

(b) All types of soil have same size of particles.

(c) Soil differ in size of particles and constituents

(d) Plants grow mostly in the bed rock

10. The Taj Mahal at Agra is a beautiful historical monument made up of pure, white marble. But, due to some causes, Taj Mahal area is discolouring its white marble and also corroding it slowly. The monument is being affected by which type of pollution?

(a) Water pollution (b) Air pollution

(c) Soil pollution (d) All of these

11. Complete the following flow chart.

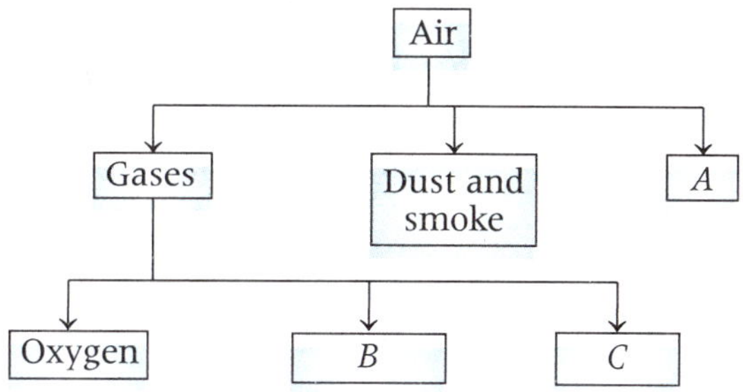

Choose the correct option.

(a) *A*–Flowers, *B*–Carbon monoxide, *C*–Hydrogen

(b) *A*–Leaves, *B*–Nitrogen, *C*–Hydrogen

(c) *A*–Water vapour, *B*–Nitrogen, *C*–Carbon dioxide

(d) *A*–Water vapour, *B*–Nitrogen, *C*–Hydrogen

12. Read the given flow chart and identify the *A*.

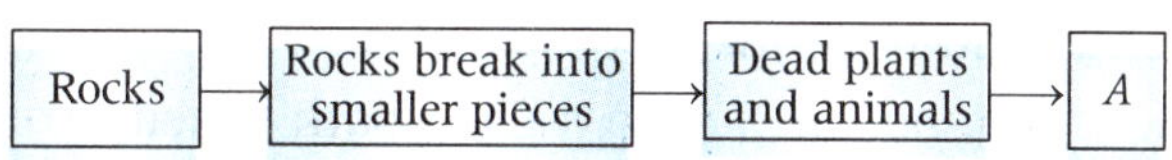

(a) Soil (b) Water (c) Air (d) Mineral

13. Salman want make an earthern pot to gift his friend. Which of the following soil, does he need to bought for pottery?

(a) Sandy soil (b) Clayey soil

(c) Loamy soil (d) All of these

14. Factory I releases toxic chemicals in a nearby river, whereas factory II releases very hot stream of water into the river. Which factor is responsible for water pollution?

(a) Factory I (b) Factory II

(c) Both I and II (d) None of these

Chapter 13

Earth and Universe

- The universe is everything we can touch, feel, sense, measure or detect. It includes living things, planets, stars, galaxies, dust clouds, light and even time.
- Our **solar system** is home to Earth and seven others planets. Each planet rotates on its own axis while revolving around the **Sun**.
- There are eight planets moving around the Sun. These are Mercury, Venus, Earth, Mars, Jupiter, Saturn, Uranus and Neptune.
- All these planets move around the Sun in a fixed path called **orbit**.
- Our solar system is part of the **milky way galaxy**.
- Smallest planet – Mercury
- Hottest planet – Venus
- Red planet – Mars
- Largest planet – Jupiter
- Coldest planet – Neptune

Sun

- The **Sun** is the nearest star to the Earth and the centre of our solar system. It is a massive ball of burning gases.
- The Sun is the main source of heat and light.

Earth

- **Earth** is the third planet from the Sun and fifth largest among the eight planets.
- The Earth is covered by layer of gases called **atmosphere**.
- The Earth also rotates on its own axis. This is called **rotation**. It takes 24 hours to complete one rotation and due to this we experience day and night.
- Earth revolves around the Sun and this movement of Earth is called **revolution**. Earth takes 365 days 6 hours or one year to complete one revolution. Due to this, we experience seasons.

Moon

- The Moon is a natural satellite of the Earth.
- It has no light of its own, but reflects the lights of the Sun.
- Changes in the shape of the Moon are called phases of the Moon.

Stars

There are millions and millions of **stars** in our galaxy and the Sun is one of those stars. They have their own light.

Constellation

- Group of stars form patterns in the sky. They are known as **constellations**, e.g. Great bear, Leo, Ursa Major, etc.
- We can see the stars, Moon and other planets from Earth by using an instrument called **telescope**.

Eclipse

- When the Sun, Moon and the Earth get aligned in the same straight line, an eclipse occurs.
- There are two major types of eclipse :
  1. **Solar Eclipse** It occurs when the Moon comes in between the Sun and the Earth.
  2. **Lunar Eclipse** It occurs when the Earth comes in between the Sun and the Moon.

Let's Practice

1. When the Earth is seen from the outer space, it looks mainly blue. This is because, most of the Earth is covered with
(a) water (b) plants (c) animals (d) air

2. The only planet with life in the solar system is
(a) Moon (b) Sun (c) Earth (d) Mars

3. The hottest planet of solar system is
(a) Saturn (b) Neptune (c) Venus (d) Mercury

4. Which one of the following heavenly bodies gives light to our solar system?

(a) 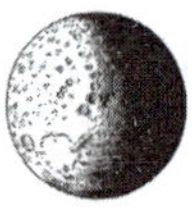
Moon

(b) 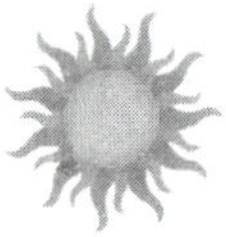
Sun

(c) 
Earth

(d) 
Saturn

5. Why there is no life on the Moon? Choose the correct option.
(a) Because Moon is a natural satellite of the Earth
(b) Because there are huge holes on the Moon called creators
(c) Because it does not have its own light
(d) Because there is no water or air on the Moon

6. Arrange the following planets in the correct sequence.
Jupiter, Earth, Mars, Venus.
(i) (ii) (iii) (iv)
(a) (iv) → (ii) → (iii) → (i) (b) (iii) → (ii) → (iv) → (i)
(c) (ii) → (iv) →(iii) → (i) (d) (i) → (ii) → (iv) → (iii)

7. Pick the odd one out.
Earth, Jupiter, Mars, Mercury, Pluto
(a) Earth (b) Mars (c) Mercury (d) Pluto

8. Study the given figure, choose the correct option for *W*, *X* and *Y*.

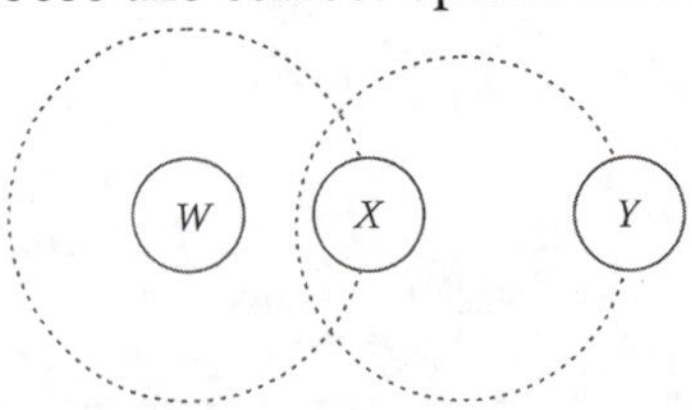

	W	*X*	*Y*		*W*	*X*	*Y*
(a)	Moon	Sun	Planet	(b)	Sun	Earth	Moon
(c)	Sun	Mars	Moon	(d)	Moon	Earth	Sun

9. The fixed path on which planet moves around the Sun is called its
(a) axis (b) rotation (c) revolution (d) orbit

10. The patterns formed by a group of stars in the sky is known as
(a) group of stars (b) full Moon (c) Sun (d) constellation

11. Which one of the following is incorrectly matched?
(a) Imaginary line about which the Earth spins–Axis
(b) A small model of the Earth – Globe
(c) An instrument helps us to see the stars, the Moon, etc. – Periscope
(d) Groups of star in a recognisable pattern in the sky–Constellations

12. Solve the riddle.

I am spherical in shape,
I made up of land, water and air,
I rotates on my axis all the time and
my rotation causes day and night.

Who am I ?
(a) Earth (b) Ball (c) Moon (d) Sun

13. Read the sentence and unscramble the given word. The spinning movement of the Earth on its axis is called

T	A	O	I	T	N	R	O

(a) Revolution (b) Rotates (c) Atmosphere (d) Rotation

14. State the following statements as true (T) or false (F).
I. Stars have their own light. II. The Moon is the natural satellite of the Earth.
(a) Both statements are true (b) Only statement I is true
(c) Only statement II is true (d) Both statements are false

15. What is the importance of Sun to us?
(a) It gives us light to see things around (b) It helps plants to make food
(c) It gives light to stars (d) Both (a) and (b)

16. Name the planet in each of the following case.
...*A*... is the biggest planet of the solar system.
...*B*... is the planet with well-developed rings around it.
Choose the correct option.
(a) *A*–Saturn, *B*–Neptune (b) *A*–Jupiter, B–Neptune
(c) *A*–Jupiter, *B*–Uranus (d) *A*–Jupiter, B–Saturn

17. Arrange the following in the increasing order - the sizes of the Earth, the Moon and the Sun.

Earth Moon Sun

(A) (B) (C)

(a) $C \to A \to B$ (b) $B \to C \to A$ (c) $A \to B \to C$ (d) $B \to A \to C$

18. Study the given Venn diagram and identify *X* and *Y*.

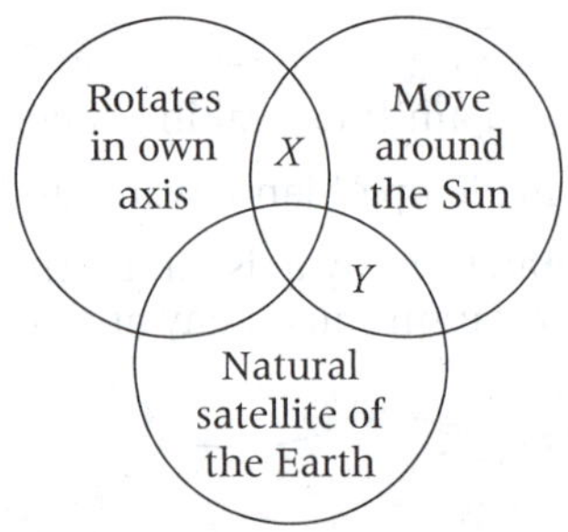

	X	*Y*
(a)	Moon	Mercury
(b)	Sun	Earth
(c)	Earth	Moon
(d)	Jupiter	Earth

19. Complete the given flow chart.

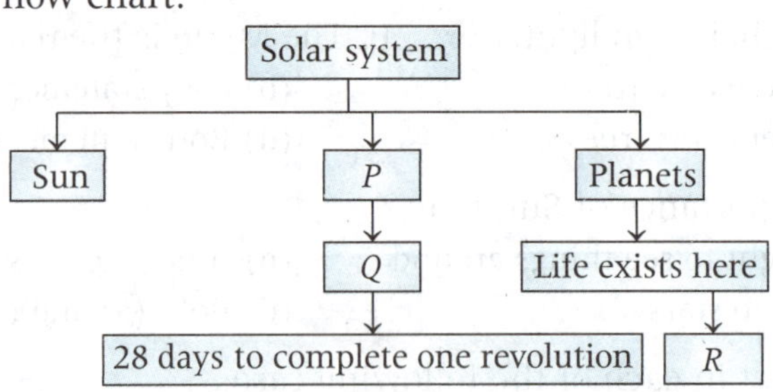

	P	*Q*	*R*
(a)	Man-made satellite	Earth	Moon
(b)	Moon	Natural satellite	Earth
(c)	Man-made satellite	Moon	Earth
(d)	Natural satellite	Earth	Moon

PRACTICE SET 01

1. Which of the following shows that living things grow in size?

A. 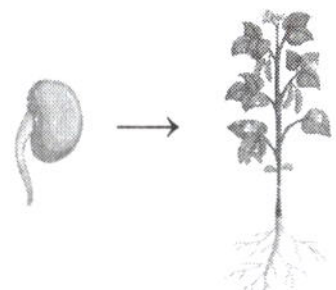 B. 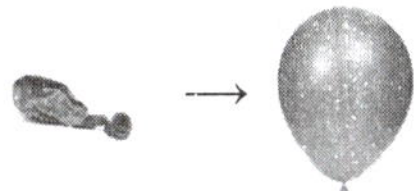 C. 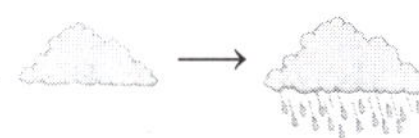 D. 

(a) A and B (b) A and D (c) B and C (d) A, C and D

2. Match the following columns.

Column I	Column II
A. 	1. Help bird to climb tree.
B. 	2. Help bird to dig out ground.
C. 	3. Help birds in swimming.
D. 	4. Help birds to catch small bi:ds.

Codes

	A	B	C	D		A	B	C	D
(a)	3	1	2	4	(b)	2	3	1	4
(c)	3	2	1	4	(d)	3	4	2	1

3. Which of the following is/are not the functions of the roots?

A. To make food for the plant. B. To take the water for the plant.

C. To hold the plant firmly to the ground.

(a) Only A (b) A and C (c) B and C (d) A, B and C

4. Fill the correct option in the blanks provided.

I. An instrument used to measure temperature is called ....

II. The normal body temperature of our body is ....°F.

(a) measurement, 98° F (b) capacity, 98.2 °F (c) thermometer, 98.6°F (d) capacity, 98.5 °F

5. Ameen wished to make water from ice. So, he started heating ice cubes on gas stove. His mother asked him to put ice cubes in the Sun instead. This saves fuel and creates no pollution. What value do you acquire?

(a) Wise use of Sun's energy
(b) Wise use of ice
(c) Wise use of gas stove
(d) Wise use of water

6. Which of the following statements about the circulatory system are correct?

I. The heart beats when it is working.
II. Blood is brought to every part of the body.
III. The circulatory system carries wastes away from all parts of the body.

(a) I and II
(b) I and III
(c) II and III
(d) I, II and III

7. Look at the given alongside picture and choose the correct option. What happen when water vapour is cooled?

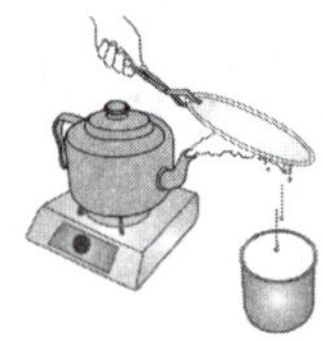

(a) Water vapour freezes
(b) Water vapour changes into water
(c) Both (a) and (b)
(d) None of these

8. Look at the pictures of following birds.

(a) (b) (c)

Which statement is true about all the birds?

(a) They have webbed feet
(b) They are flightless bird
(c) They can swim and fly
(d) They have feathers covering their bodies

9. Read the clues and fill the correct word.

I. The change of water into water vapour ....
II. The change of water vapour into water ....

	I	II
(a)	Cooling	Boiling
(b)	Freezing	Heating
(c)	Evaporation	Condensation
(d)	Condensation	Evaporation

10. In the system shown below, digestion does not take place in the organ labelled...... .

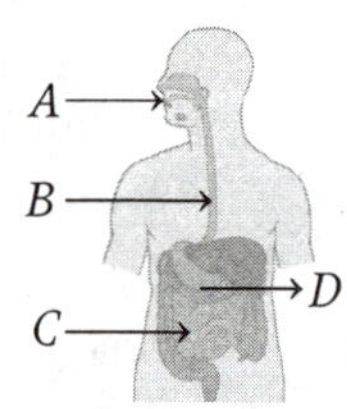

(a) *A*
(b) *B*
(c) *C*
(d) *D*

11. Guess my name.
I am a group of stars that can be seen only in night sky. When seen in the night sky, I look like a great bear. Who am I?
(a) Star (b) Milky way galaxy (c) Comet (d) Constellation

12. Match the following columns.

	Column I		Column II
A.	Multi-storeyed building	1.	Winter season
B.	Woolen clothes	2.	A house on wheels
C.	Caravan	3.	House made on long pieces of wood
D.	Stilt	4.	Many floors

Codes

	A	B	C	D		A	B	C	D
(a)	4	1	3	2	(b)	1	2	4	3
(c)	4	1	2	3	(d)	3	4	2	1

13. Select the non-living thing.
(a) butterfly (b) bird (c) dog (d) weather

14. The main purpose of plant's flower is
(a) provide support (b) provide water (c) produce seeds (d) produce food

15. During solar eclipse ...*X*... comes between ...*Y*... and ...*Z*... .

	X	*Y*	*Z*		*X*	*Y*	*Z*
(a)	Sun	Moon	Earth	(b)	Sun	Earth	Moon
(c)	Moon	Sun	Earth	(d)	Earth	Moon	Sun

16. How many bones are present in human body?
(a) 203 (b) 205 (c) 206 (d) 200

17. On which day can a rainbow be formed in the sky?
(a) Sunny and windy (b) Cloudy and windy (c) Rainy and sunny (d) Sunny and cloudy

18. Which one of the following is the standard unit for the measurement of time?
(a) Second (b) Minute (c) Hour (d) All of these

19. Soil is made up of
(a) pieces of rocks (b) air and water
(c) matter that was once alive (d) All of these

20. Which of the given animals is not domesticated by human beings?

(a) 
(b) 
(c) 
(d) 

21. State which statement(s) is/are incorrect.

I. Food provide nourishment to our body. II. We get food only from plants.

III. Different culture has different type of food.

Choose the correct option.

(a) I and II (b) Only II (c) Only III (d) I and III

22. The matter that easily spread into the air

(a) solid (b) gas (c) liquid (d) None of these

23. A man is moving in a straight line. Which type of motion does he follows?

(a) Non-uniform motion (b) Periodic motion

(c) Linear motion (d) Uniform motion

24. Which of the following gives green colour of plants?

(a) Carbohydrate (b) Fat (c) Chlorophyll (d) Vitamin

25. Read the statements given by four children and select the one who made a correct statement.

(a) A carpenter makes old and torn shoes and also make new shoes.

(b) A policeman manages traffic on road.

(c) A barber cuts our hair by using comb and scissors.

(d) A potter makes things out of wood for us like doors.

26. 'Living thing can move' based on this statement identify the incorrect statement/s from the option given below

I. Car can move its a living thing. II. Cow can move, its a living thing.

III. Children can run they are living thing. IV. Clouds can move they are living thing.

Choose the correct option.

(a) Statement I only (b) Statements I and IV (c) Statement IV only (d) Statement III only

27. In the given Venn diagram which describe the lion.

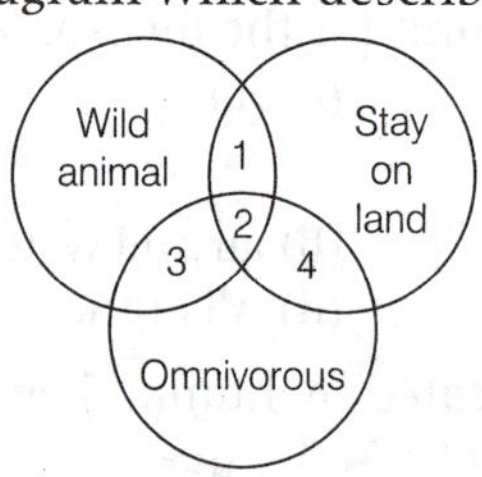

A

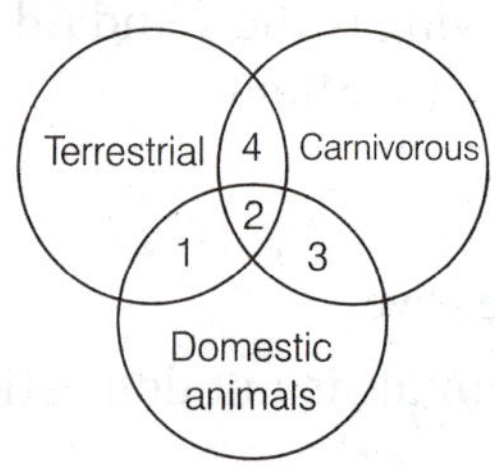

B

	A	B
(a)	1	4
(b)	1	2
(c)	1	3
(d)	2	4

28. Which of these is not a modified root?
(a) Turnip (b) Carrot (c) Radish (d) Potato

29.
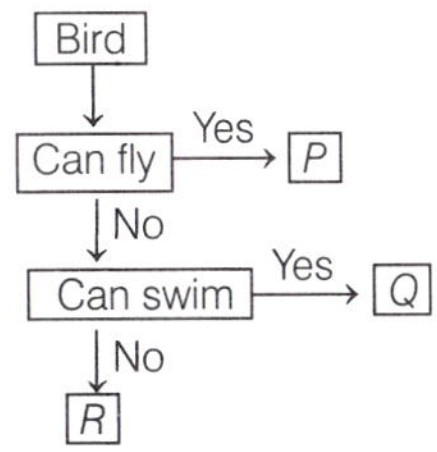

Complete the flow chart and choose the correct option for *P*, *Q* and *R*.

	P	*Q*	*R*
(a)	Penguin	Pigeon	Ostrich
(b)	Pigeon	Penguin	Ostrich
(c)	Kingfisher	Pigeon	Penguin
(d)	Penguin	Ostrich	Kingfisher

30. Which type of soil is tightly packed with tiny grains?
(a) Humus (b) Sandy soil (c) Loamy soil (d) Clayey soil

31. Mark the correct option.
(a) Solid-juice, wood
(b) Liquid-stone, hammer
(c) Gas-coffee, tang
(d) Matter-water, air

32. Refer to Venn diagram, identify *X* and *Y*.
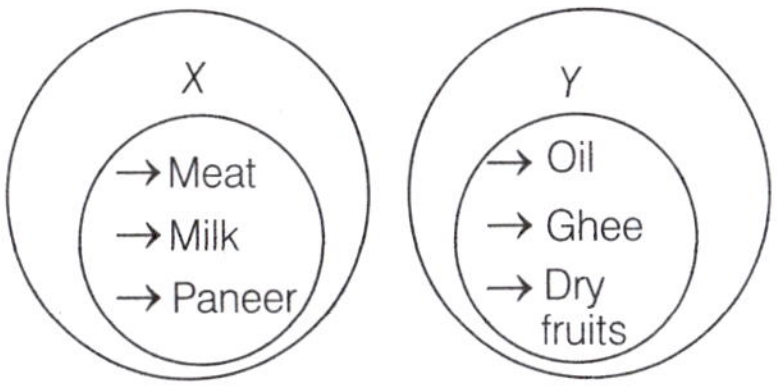

	X	*Y*
(a)	Protein	Carbohydrates
(b)	Carbohydrates	Fat
(c)	Vitamin	Fat
(d)	Protein	Fat

33. The voice box help us to speak, make sounds. Where is it found?
(a) Rib (b) Heart (c) Lungs (d) Throat

34. Which bird from the following has a beak to suck nectar from flowers?
(a) Parrot (b) Duck (c) Hummingbird (d) Sparrow

35. Cloud formation take place due to
(a) condensation
(b) evaporation
(c) precipitation
(d) Both (a) and (b)

PRACTICE SET 02

1. Look at the figure given below.

The Earth rotates on its fixed imaginary axis

What results with the above motion of the Earth?
(a) Change of season (b) Formation of day and night (c) Full moon (d) Amavasya

2. Which one of the following statement is correct?
(a) The leaf absorbs water and minerals for the plant
(b) The leaf helps to hold the plant firmly to the ground
(c) The leaf is where the exchange of gases happens for the plant
(d) The roots help to hold the plant upright

3. Study the human skeletal system shown in figure.

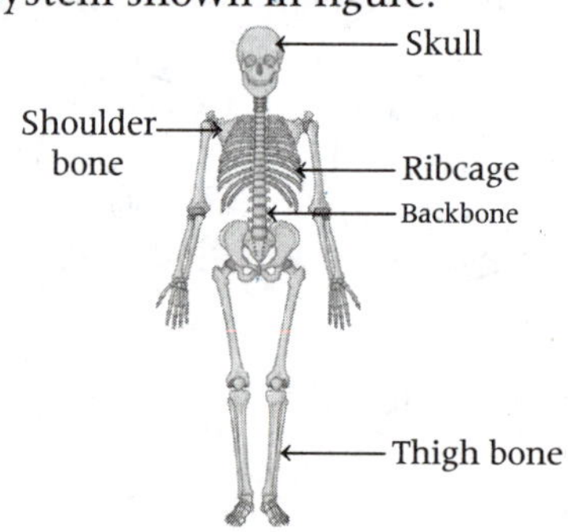

Which of the following correctly matches the organ to the part of the skeletal system protecting it?

	Brain is protected by	Heart is protected by
(a)	Skull	Backbone
(b)	Head	Thigh bone
(c)	Skull	Ribcage
(d)	Head	Shoulder bone

4. Which of the following animals feed on plants or animals or both?

A.  B.  C.  D. 

(a) A and B (b) B and D (c) C and D (d) B, C and D

5. Write the time taken for one.

I. Rotation of the Earth on its axis...... . II. Revolution of the Earth around the Sun ....

III. Rotation of the Moon around the Earth ....

(a) 24 hours, 365 days, 29 days (b) 28 days, 24 hours, 65 days

(c) 365 days, 24 hours, 29 days (d) 24 hours,28 days, 365 days

6. Choose the incorrect statement.

(a) We should wash the fruits and vegetables well before we eat them

(b) We should throw the waste/stale food around

(c) We should eat our food at regular intervals

(d) We should always eat freshly cooked food

7. What cause changes in season?

(a) Rotation of the Earth on its own axis (b) Revolution of Moon around the Sun

(c) Revolution of the Earth around the Sun (d) Revolution of Sun around the Moon

8. You bought a packet of juice from the market. It has a label which says 1 L. What does it signify?

(a) Volume (b) Length (c) Weight (d) Time

9. Heart is a part of

(a) muscular system (b) nervous system (c) excretory system (d) circulatory system

10. Complete the following food chain by filling the correct option.

Grass ⟶ *A* ⟶ Frog ⟶ *B* ⟶ Eagle

(a) Deer, Tiger (b) Cow, Lion (c) Grasshopper, Snake (d) Deer, Snake

11. Study the table and answer the question.

Animals		
Group *A*	**Group *B***	**Group *C***
Zebra	Duck	Molly
Human	Eagle	Seahorse
Cat	Pelican	Swordtail

What could be group *A*, *B* and *C* ?

(a) Mammals, Birds, Fish (b) Mammals, Insects, Birds

(c) Birds, Fish, Mammals (d) Mammals, Birds, Insects

12. The given food items *A* and *B* are .... and ....

A

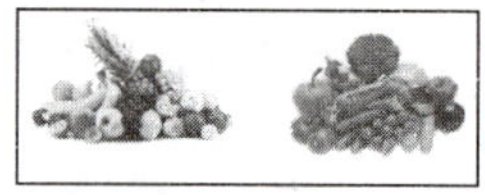

B

	Food item *A*	Food item *B*
(a)	Protective food	Roughage
(b)	Energy giving food	Protective food
(c)	Body building food	Energy giving food
(d)	Energy giving food	Body building food

13. Select the plant among the following in which stem stores food.
(a) Carrot (b) Ginger (c) Spinach (d) Mango

14. Pick out the natural living things .
(a) butterfly (b) mountains (c) pencil (d) river

15. The movement of the Earth around the Sun in an orbit is called

L	U	O	I	N	R	O	V	E	T

(a) atmosphere (b) revolution (c) rotation (d) astronauts

16. Planting a tree is one of the best things you can do for your local environment and for the planet because
(a) they produce oxygen
(b) they remove carbon dioxide and contaminants from the air
(c) they provide habitat for birds and other wildlife
(d) All of the above

17. Four students made a statement each about why do we need food?

Anu: Food gives us energy.
Sonu: Food is needed for growth.
Anil: It help us to stay healthy.
Rohan: It does not protect us from illness.

Which student did not make a correct statement?
(a) Anu (b) Sonu (c) Anil (d) Rohan

18. Select the odd one out, on the basis of mode of transport.

(a) 
(b) 
(c) 
(d) 

19. Two major categories in which things can be classified are
(a) man-made thing and natural
(b) living and non-living
(c) wood and plastic
(d) tools and machines

20. A girl is riding a bicycle. In the first hour, she travels 5 km, in the second hour she travels 10 km and the third hour she travels 15 km. What is the total distance travelled by her?
(a) 15 km
(b) 20 km
(c) 30 km
(d) 25 km.

21. Which of the following does not take the shape of the vessel in which it is kept?

(a) 
(b) 
(c) 
(d) 

22. Match the following columns.

Column I		Column II
A.	Sunny days	1. Clouds in the sky making the weather nice
B.	Rainy days	2. Fast moving wind blows
C.	Cloudy days	3. Welcomed by farmers and children
D.	Windy days	4. Cloudless, warm and bright

Codes

	A	B	C	D
(a)	4	1	2	3
(b)	2	3	4	1
(c)	4	3	1	2
(d)	3	4	2	1

23. Chutki has taken an empty bottle and fixed a deflated balloon on its mouth. She placed the bottle in a container filled with hot water. After some time, the balloon gets inflated as shown: What could be the most appropriate reason for this?

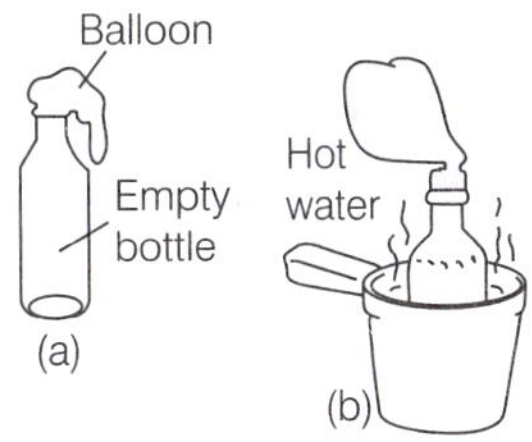

(a) Air when gets heated becomes heavier.
(b) Air when gets heated becomes lighter and settle down.
(c) Air when gets heated becomes heavier and settle down.
(d) Air when gets heated becomes lighter and rises up.

24. *X* and *Y* are two types of plants. Plant *X* has a thin, long and weak stem, which cannot stand upright on its own, but it readily moves up by a nearby support. On the other hand, plant *Y* is small-sized, having a soft and delicate stem and have a short lifespan. Plant *X* and *Y* are

	X	*Y*
(a)	Herbs	Shrubs
(b)	Shrubs	Climbers
(c)	Climbers	Herbs
(d)	Climbers	Shrubs

25. Complete the given flow chart.

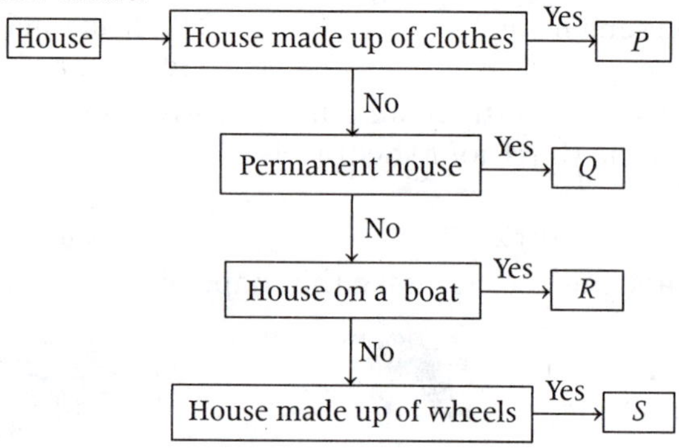

Identify *P*, *Q*, *R* and *S*.

	P	*Q*	*R*	*S*
(a)	Huts	Houseboat	Caravan	Igloo
(b)	Multistorey	Huts	Tent	Stilt house building
(c)	Tent	Bungalow	Houseboat	Caravan
(d)	Huts	Houseboat	Bungalow	Tent

26. Which of the given statement is false?

I. Birds have teeths within their beak.
II. They move their neck continuously.
III. All birds made their nests.
IV. The body of birds is coverved with feathers.

Choose the correct option.

(a) I and II (b) II and IV (c) I and III (d) Only I

27. Which sense organ will help you to find that the hot soup is salty?

(a) Eyes (b) Skin (c) Tongue (d) Both (b) and (c)

28. Complete the flow chart given and choose the correct option for *P*, *Q* and *R*.

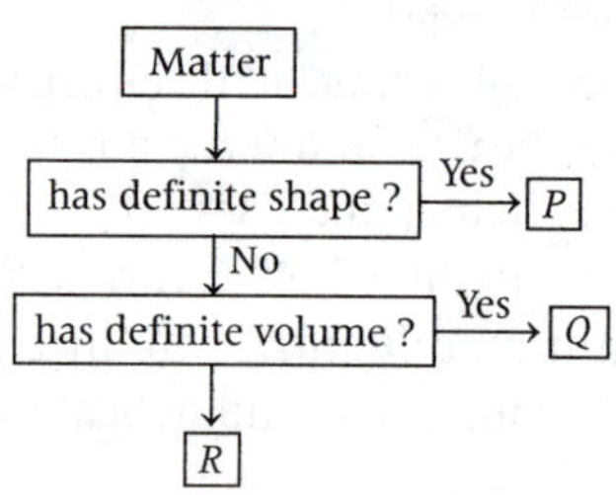

	P	*Q*	*R*
(a)	Solid	Gas	Liquid
(b)	Solid	Liquid	Gas
(c)	Gas	Liquid	Solid
(d)	Liquid	Solid	Gas

29. State the following statements for True (T) and False (F).

I. Muscular system protects the inner delicate organs of our body.
II. Digestive system consists of nose, windpipe and lungs.

Choose the correct option.

	I	II		I	II
(a)	F	T	(b)	T	F
(c)	F	F	(d)	T	T

30. Which of the following statement is false?
(a) Herbivores are animals that eat plants and parts of plants
(b) They have flat broad front teeth to cut the leaves and grasses
(c) They chew the food with the help of strong back teeth
(d) Some examples of herbivores are tiger, lion, leopard

31. A car is moving on a straight road with uniform motion. In the first hour, it travels 60 km. How much distance it will cover in next 1 hour?

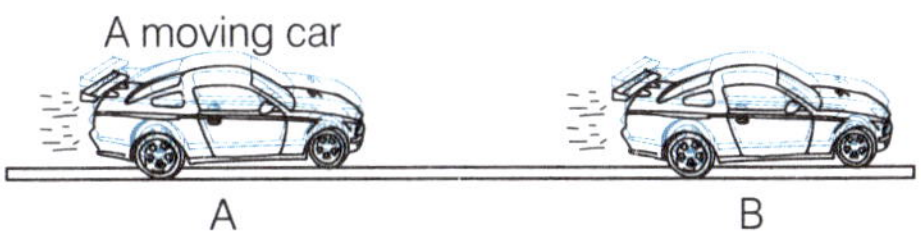

(a) 50 km (b) 60 km (c) 45 km (d) 55 km

32. Which controls all our activities of seeing, hearing, learning, thinking and feeling?
(a) Skeletal system (b) Nervous system
(c) Excretory system (d) Circulatory system

33. Identify the correct relation

Hoopoe : ___*A*___ : : ___*B*___ : hooked

	A	*B*		*A*	*B*
(a)	Chisel-shaped	Parrot	(b)	Broad and flat	Vulture
(c)	Short, strong	Crow	(d)	Chisel-shaped	Eagle

34. The given diagram shows the length of the shadow as double the height of the object.

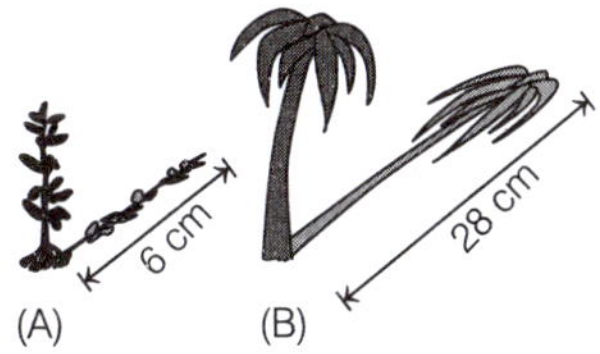

Find the height of the both trees.

	A	B
(a)	6 cm	28 cm
(b)	4 cm	16 cm
(c)	3 cm	14 cm
(d)	5 cm	20 cm

35. In the food chain given below
Grass → Deer → Tiger
The deer is a
(a) producer (b) consumer (c) Both (a) and (b) (d) None of these

Hints & Solutions

Living and Non-living Things

1. (*c*) Option (c) is correct because mountain and river are natural non-living things and table is a man-made, non-living thing. Only plant is the living thing.
2. (*a*) River is natural, non-living thing, while all other options, i.e. plant, tree and children are living things.
3. (*d*) All the given options are the examples of non-living things made by humans.
4. (*c*) Bag is made up of jute , sweater is made up of wool and basket is made up of bamboo but bottel is made up of plastic. Hence, it is not made up of natural thing.
5. (*b*) Living things need both **food** and **water** to survive.
6. (*a*) If a living thing get food but no water and air, it will die because living thing need food, air and water to survive.
7. (*b*) Living things take in air to breath.
8. (*d*) Rock is a non-living thing, they do not reproduce, hence option (d) is odd.
9. (*d*) Animals need air, water and food from environment for their survival.
10. (*b*) The development of seed into plant shows its growth. Growth is the characteristic of all living things.
11. (*d*) All the living things can breath, reproduce and need food and water except walking. Because, plants cannot move from one place to another by their own but are living things.
12. (*a*) Sunflower shows movement by turning towards the Sun.
13. (*c*) Toys are man-made non-living things, whereas mountain, valleys and rivers are natural non-living things.
14. (*a*) Plants can make their own food, but a dog either prey or depend on its owner.
15. (*a*) We all need food to grow. A table in your room cannot move on its own as it is a non-living thing. Plants needs sunlight, air and water to prepare their food.
16. (*c*) Here, *X*-contains non-living things
    Y-contains living things and
    Z-also contains living things.
17. (*b*) Monu and Golu made incorrect statements because all non-living things are not man-made some are natural. All living things cannot make their own food only plants can make it.
18. (*d*) All living things grow on their own.
    A stone cannot walk on its own. plants are living things but cannot move from one place to another, they show movement by turning or bending towards light.
19. (*b*) Car is a man-made non-living thing. It cannot grow, reproduce, breath or move on its own.

Plants

1. (*c*) Stem carries food and water to different parts of the plant. It passes water and minerals from the roots to other parts of the plants. It also passes food made by the leaves to other parts of the plants.
2. (*d*) Carrot and turnip both are root of the vegetables.
3. (*b*) Sugarcane and potato are the stem, while carrot is a root and tomato is a fruit.
4. (*d*) Grass can be pulled out from the soil most easily because they have very small roots.
5. (*d*) Only tree III will bear fruit as it is a coconut tree. Others are I-banyan tree, II-pine tree and IV-*Cactus* plant.
6. (*b*) Stem of sugarcane is edible.
7. (*a*) 'A' is **root**. The plant part which we eat in a cabbage are its leaves and the plant part which we eat in radish plant is its root.
8. (*a*) Green leaves of a plant helps them in making their own food. Since, mushrooms does not have green leaves, therefore they cannot make their own food.
9. (*a*) Leaves are known as food factory.
    - Roots helps in the absorption of minerals.
    - Flowers develop into fruits.
    - Fruits protect seeds.
10. (*c*) Root fixes the plant in the soil.
    Stem or bark takes water from the roots to the leaf. Leaves make food for the plant.
    Flower changes into fruits. Sprouted seed grows into a new tree.

11. (*a*) Rose is an example of shrubs.
- Grass is an example of herbs.
- Grapevine is an example of climbers.
- Money plant is an example of creepers.

12. (*a*) Incorrect statements can be corrected as
(i) Plants are living things.
(ii) Climbers need support to stand as they have weak stems.
(iii) Money plant is not a big plant, it is a climbers.

13. (*c*) Plants like sugarcane, extra food is stored in the stem and in plants like the potato and ginger, the stem grows underground and stores extra food. Hence, correct answer is option (c), we eat stem of sugarcane and potato.

14. (*d*) Both Arjun and Rakhi are wrong as all leaves of a plant are of same shape. Also roots (not leaves) hold the plant firmly in the soil.

15. (*a*) Plants need water to survive. Leaves make food for the plants, so it uses sunlight, air and water to make food for plants.
Here, Sonal forgot one thing that is watering the plant.

16. (*c*) Part *Y*, i.e. stem support the leaves and carries the food made by the leaves to the rest of the plants.

17. (*b*) If all the leaves and roots are removed from a plant, it will die eventually. Thus, option with plants *B* and *D* is correct.

18. (*b*) Stem of *Cactus* plant makes and stores food as its leaves are modified into spines.

19. (*b*) The leaves of *Cactus* plant is small and needle like so as to reduce water loss due to harsh dry condition of desert.

20. (*d*) Peepal leaves are triangular. Lotus leaves are round. Guava leaves are oblong to oval in shape. *Cactus* leaves hereturned into small and needle-like structures called spine.

Animals

1. (*c*) Animals which live on land are called terrestrial animals. Dog and tiger are the terrestrial animals.

2. (*b*) Pig and rat are the animals which feed on plants and animals both. The animals which eat both plants and animals are called omnivores.
Giraffe (I) is a herbivore, while lion (III) is a carnivore (which eat only animals).

3. (*c*) Elephant likes to eat the sugarcane.
Horse loves to eat grasses.
Cat likes to eat mouse.
Rabbit likes to eat carrot.

4. (*d*) All the options are correct except option, i.e. (d) frog swallow their food as a whole.

5. (*c*) Pet animals live with humans, e.g. dog, cat.
Domestic animals are useful to mankind, e.g. cow, sheep, goat, etc.

6. (*c*) *X* - Carnivorous, *Y* - Omnivorous
Z - Herbivorous

7. (*c*) A Jaguar has limbs, but a fish does not have wings.

8. (*b*) Here, animals are classified according to their habitats. The animals in group A live in water, while the animals in group B live on land. In group B, the dolphin is a fish and lives in water, so it has been grouped wrongly.

9. (*a*) I. Cow, buffalo, camel and horse are cud-chewing animals. They chew their food after eating.
II. Kangaroo, zebra and deer are herbivores.
III. Food keeps animal healthy and strong .
IV. A mosquito has a long tube to suck blood.

10. (*c*) An aquarium is home for fish. It is a small ecosystem in which fishes are able to get their food, shelter and live happily.

11. (*c*)(i) Frog has a long sticky tongue.
(ii) Earthworm swallow soil.
(iii) Mosquito suck blood.
(iv) Donkey carries loads for us.

12. (*b*) Gills (*A*) of fish use for respiration.
- Scales (*B*) helps in swimming and protect fish from predators and parasites.
- Fin (*C*) helps to swim.
- Tail fin (*D*) helps to propel and move forward while swimming.

13. (*b*) A bear lives on land and shark have fins and tail. In option (a), giraffe live on land, but dolphin do not have fins. In option (c), tiger and cat both lives on land. In option (d), dolphin lives in water and zebra do not have fins.

14. (*a*) By unscrambling the letters we get, the name of animal, i.e. butterfly, it sucks nectar from flowers.

15. (*c*) **Terrestrial** animals are those that live on the land. They have **legs** to walk and have well-developed **sense** organs. Their claws and **teeth** are very sharp which enables them to catch and eat their prey.
16. (*d*) The food chain shows how plants are eaten by animals and animals are eaten by other animals. Food chain can be completed as Grass → Grasshopper → Frog → Eagle → Snake.

Birds

1. (*a*) Sunbird has long and pointed beak through which she suck the nectar of different flowers.
2. (*d*) Chisel-shaped beak is used to make holes in the tree.
3. (*c*) Hen has three toes on front and one on back which helps in scraching the ground.
4. (*b*) Ostrich lays the biggest egg in the world.
5. (*b*) Crow has two toes on front and two toes on back which help them to hold the branches.
6. (*a*) The tailor bird has a beak like a sewing needle. It uses its beak to sew leaves to make nest.
7. (*b*) Birds like emu, turkey and penguin do not fly but humming bird can fly.
8. (*d*) Woodpecker is a climbing bird. They have two toes pointing forward and two pointing backward which help them to climb on trunk of tree.
9. (*c*) Eagle - Strong and hooked beak to tear flesh.
   Goose - Broad and flat beak with holes to find insect in muddy water.
   Parrot - Curved beak to break hard nuts.
   Hoopoe - Chisel-shaped to make hole in tree trunk.
10. (*b*) Parrot is of green colour and has curved beak to crack nuts and seeds, whereas the duck is of white colour and has broad and flat beak.
11. (*a*) Only option (a) is correct. Other options can be corrected as.
    Tailor bird use its needle-like beak to make their nest.
    Vulture and eagles make their nest in shape of shallow cup. Woodpecker pecks at a tree to make their nest.
12. (*a*) Bats are mammals that have wings and can fly. They are not birds because they give birth to young ones and do not have beaks or feathers.
13. (*b*) A woodpecker has strong and chisel-shaped beak to make hole in wood and pull out insects, while a sunbird has long and pointed beak to suck the nectar of flowers.
14. (*d*) Penguin they live in cold and icy place they are flight less birds.
15. (*d*) As mentioned in the passage, the Para-Para has a beak and its outer covering is feathers. Para-Para can fly.
16. (*b*) Anil did not make a correct statement. Ostrich is a bird, which cannot fly. It lays eggs and have feathers also.
17. (*b*) Tailor bird has long pointed needle-like beak through which she sew her nest made up of palm and banana leaves.
18. (*c*) *A* - Flesh eating bird like vulture or eagle.
    B- Climbing bird like woodpecker.
    C - Scratching bird like hen.
19. (*b*) Swan can fly and swim comfortably whereas owl and parrot can fly but cannot swim and ostrich cannot fly or swim.

Human Body

1. (*b*) Nose helps us in smelling things.
2. (*c*) The heart rate of a healthy person is 72 times per minute.
3. (*b*) Our sense of **touch** and **taste** tells us that food is hot and tasty.
4. (*d*) Brain is protected by the skull. Skull is the hard braincase, which does not affect the brain whenever injury takes place.
5. (*d*) The process of taking in oxygen and giving out carbon dioxide is called breathing.
6. (*c*) Circulatory system helps to carry blood to all parts of our body.
7. (*d*) The *X* in the given figure is windpipe through which the air moves down to the lungs.
8. (*c*) The function of heart is to pump blood.
9. (*a*) Both the given statements are correct as, There are 206 bones in human body and two or more bones are connected together to form joints. Joints allow as to twist or bend our body.
10. (*c*) The correct sequence of organ through which air will pass is
    Nose → Windpipe → Lungs → All parts of body.
11. (*c*) **Nervous** *system* control all action of our body.
12. (*b*) Stomach is a part of digestive system and skeleton system comprises of bones.

13. (*d*) The organ send messages to brain through nerves. Nervous system controls all the actions of our body.

14. (*b*) Kidneys are the part of excretory system. Carbon dioxide is the product of respiratory system. We inhaled oxygen in return we exhaled out carbon dioxide. Nerves belong to the nervous system. Food pipe belongs to the digestive system.

15. (*d*) Rohan got injured and broke his ribcage. The function of ribcage is to protect the vital organs such as heart, lungs and liver. According to the options, heart and lungs are in danger.

16. (*d*) The skeletal system is composed of bones, which give shape and support to the body. It protects the internal, delicate and soft organs from injury.

17. (*c*) In the given Venn diagram '*P*' is lungs because lungs is an organ of respiration and also the organ of excretion as it remove carbon dioxide from the body.

18. (*c*) Option (c) is correct
X -Digestive system helps in digestion of food.
Y - Circulatory system helps in transfer of blood from heart to all parts of our body.
Z - Excretory system helps in removal of waste substance from our body.

Food

1. (*d*) Honey is the animal product we get honey from honeybees.

2. (*d*) People living in Tamil Nadu eat idli and dosa.

3. (*a*) Plant gives us pulses, vegetables, nuts etc.

4. (*d*) Protein : Meat :: Fat : Ghee
Meat is source of protein and ghee is a source of fat.

5. (*d*) Curd, butter and cream are prepared from cow's milk. Honey is obtained from honeybee.

6. (*c*) Burger, pizzas, popcorn, ice cream, etc., are examples of junk food. They do not have nutritive value. These make a person obese.

7. (*d*) Fats are found in olive oil, peanut oil, fish oils, soybean oil, corn, sunflower, cotton seed and cooking oils.

8. (*b*) Carbohydrates are found in greatest quantities in rice, chappatis, potatoes, bread, bananas, pear, corn, beans.
These food items provide us energy. Some of these are not source of protein, i.e. banana and potato.

9. (*b*) Growing, children should eat body building food, i.e. protein rich food as it helps in growth and development of the body.

10. (*c*) Minerals like calcium are essential for the formation of teeth and bone.

11. (*c*) When a person is fasting its body get energy from the fat which is stored in its body.

12. (*a*) Eating food, while talking and laughing is not a healthy eating habit.

13. (*c*) I. Fruits and vegetables keep the eyes, bones and teeth healthy.
II. They also protect us from illness.
III. These vegetables do not give instant energy, because instant energy is given by carbohydrates.
IV. These foods have nutrient value.

14. (*c*) Plate of student III contain right nutrients in it because there is no junk food in his plate.

15. (*c*) All the given statements are correct
I. Some food can be eaten raw without cooking like, fruit and vegetables.
II. Most of the food items need to be cooked before they can be eaten.
III. Cooking makes the food tasty, healthy and digestible.

16. (*b*) Turmeric is used a lot in Indian cooking. It is used as an antiseptic also. It is yellow in colour.

Housing, Clothing and Occupation

1. (*a*) Hut is known as kachcha house.

2. (*b*) Stilt house made on wooden poles. They are suitable for place like Assam, where it rains heavily and floods are common.

3. (*a*) Bricks are hard and strong.

4. (*c*) Cotton fibre is obtained from cotton plant.

5. (*d*) Woolen shawl is made from wool.

6. (*d*) A tent house is made up of canvas. It can be folded, can carried along easily.
Campers, nomads, soldiers and construction workers use this type of house.

7. (*d*) Igloo is found in cold countries and eskimos live in these houses.
Stilt is a house made on long pieces of wood or metal.
A caravan is a house on wheels.
A wooden house made on a boat is called a houseboat.

8. (*a*) A hut is made up of mud and water.
An igloo is made up of snow.

A houseboat is made up of wood.
A tent house is made up of canvas.

9. *(a)* In ice cold places people cut blocks of snow to make house called igloos.
10. *(c)* Waterproof materials are used in an umbrella, because they does not leak water.
11. *(c)* Caravan is a house on wheels. It can be moved from place to place.
12. *(c)* In month of December, that means in winter, we usually wear dark coloured clothes made from wool that do not allow the body heat to escape.
13. *(d)* The materials shown in picture are bricks and cement. They are used to make strong and permanent house called pakka house.
14. *(d)* People who keep moving from one place to another live in temporary house like caravans, tents, etc.
15. *(c)* Antartica is a cold region, so Divya would wear sweater there.
16. *(d)* In the given figure (1) and (2) are permanent house. While figure (3) is a tent, i.e. temporary house.
17. *(c)* Sunlight keeps the rooms free from germs. Chimneys let the smoke go out.
Verandah is used to sit and enjoy the fresh air and warmth of sunlight.
Wire netting keeps the mosquitoes and flies away.
18. *(b)* Doctor use stethoscope. Weighmachine used by shopkeeper, spud (khurpa) is used by farmer, screw is used by plumber or someone who maintain machine and engines, etc.
19. *(c)* Here, *'P'* could be a policeman, *'Q'* could be a mechanic and *'R'* could be a doctor.

Water and Weather

1. *(b)* Rain is the natural source of pure water. Sea and oceans have salt water and ponds are dirty.
2. *(c)* The process of converting of water into vapour is called evaporation.
3. *(d)* Water cycle is describe as the continuous movement of water on above and below the surface of Earth.
The correct process of water cycle is evaporation, condensation, precipitation and collection.
4. *(c)* The condition of air at particular place and at a particular time is called weather. Weather keeps on changing.
5. *(d)* Wet clothes dry faster on sunny and windy day as rate of evaporation is faster on these day.
6. *(d)* The weather depends on the Sun, the wind, the clouds and the rain. So, all these factors can affect the weather.
7. *(d)* There are five seasons in a year, i.e. summer, monsoon (rainy season), autumn, winter, spring.
8. *(b)* In summers, we need to drink plenty of water as we lose a lot of it, while sweating.
9. *(d)* In spring season, the weather is pleasant, because trees have new green leaves and new flowers bloom with butterflies.
10. *(a)* The clothes in summer dry faster than in winters because of high evaporation in summers.
11. *(c)* Both the statements are true.
Lack of rain over a long period of time result in drought. Too much rain causes flood.
12. *(c)* Ice on melting turns into water which further on evaporation converts into water vapours.
13. *(b)* Only statement (I) is correct and statements (II) and (III) are incorrect because weather changes from place to place and weather changes many times in a day and night also.
14. *(d)* Winter is the coldest time of the year. In this season, fog and storm occur which can cause accidents, hence travel, outing and sports become difficult during winter season.
15. *(d)* The water vapour present in air is called humidity. It is highest in the rainy season.

Matter and Materials

1. *(a)* Steam can be defined as gas and chair can be defined as solid.
2. *(c)* Milk is liquid, others are solid.
3. *(a)* When solid converts to liquid, it is known as melting.
4. *(d)* Water is found in all 3 states of matter.
5. *(a)* Balloon *A* (when blown) is heavier because it has the weight of the balloon and also the air inside it and balloon *B* (when not blown) has only the weight of balloon and not of air.
6. *(b)* In the given list, solids are eraser, paper, book, chair, laptop.
Liquids are water, juice, oil, coffee.

7. *(d)* Liquid has definite volume but does not has definite shape.

8. *(c)*

A. Knife	–	Metal	(2)
B. Mirror	–	Glass	(4)
C. Wooden door	–	Tree	(1)
D. Rubber tyre	–	Rubber	(3)

Knife is made up of metal. Mirror is made up of glass. Wooden door is made up of tree and rubber tyre is made up of rubber.

9. *(a)* We can smell a perfume in the nearby room because the molecule of perfume are very loose and flow easily.

10. *(d)* Vapours is gaseous state. Hence, option (d) is incorrect. Some other gaseous states are smog, steam etc.

11. *(c)* After sometime, some amount of water will evaporate and the amount of water will become less.

12. *(d)* Umbrella is waterproof and rubber band is stretchy.

13. *(a)* Here, the complete flow chart is

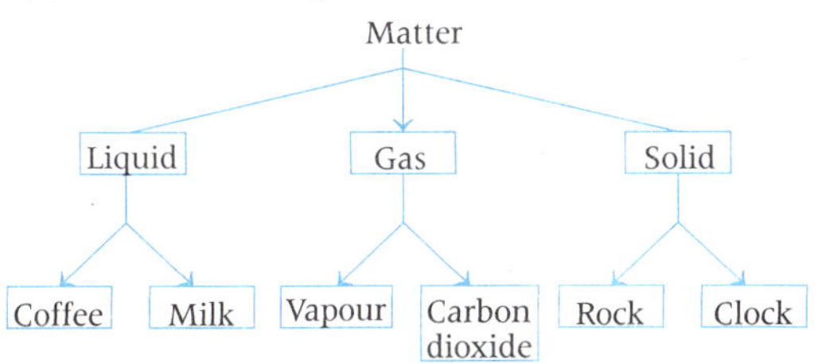

14. *(c)* The pattern followed in given series is solid : liquid : gas.

15. *(d)* As both Piyush and Komal can see each other, the sheet *X* should be transparent. Among the given option, only glass is transparent.

16. *(b)* As water did not collect in the container it means that the material '*X*' is glass, which does not allow water to pass through it. Cloth, paper and cardboard allow water to pass through them.

Measurements

1. *(c)* Clothes are measured with a ruler (scale).

2. *(c)* The weight (mass) of an object is measured using a balance.

3. *(a)* The amount of liquid (a container can hold) is capacity.

4. *(b)* For finding the temperature at which water boils we use thermometer.

5. *(d)* Option (d) is correct as milk in a bottle can be measured by using a measuring cylinder and sugar in a bowl can be measured by electronic balance.
Therefore, these can be measured easily.
Other options like width of hair and air around us cannot be measured easily.

6. *(c)* I. Fruits are measured in kilogram (kg).
II. Cold drink can be measured in millilitre (mL).
III. Cloth for a shirt is measured in metre (m).
IV. Time is measured in second (s).

7. *(d)* Length of a room is measured in metre. Volume of milk is measured by measuring can. Mass of a book is measured in kilogram. Temperature on a cold day can be measured in °C.

8. *(c)* Things which are smaller in length are measured in centimetre and metre ruler or measuring tape is used to measure length.

9. *(c)* Standard unit for measuring length is not centimetre, but metre it is the standard unit for measuring length. So, option (c) is the incorrect statement.

10. *(a)* A measuring tape is used to measure the length of a cloth. Watch is used to measure the time. Weighing balance are used to measure weight and measuring cylinder is used to measure volume.

11. *(c)* I. The smaller container, the lesser will be its capacity to hold liquids.
II. Temperature is the measure of coldness or hotness of an object.
Therefore, both statements are true.

12. *(b)* The distance from Salman school to home is measured in km.

13. *(b)* Ritika finishes her homework in less time i.e. 40 minutes while Rhea took 1 hr i.e. 60 minutes to complete her homework.

14. *(d)* As the number of steps of Shivani is more than other children. This means she has the shortest step.

15. *(b)* Length of ribbon left will be 40 m, because Sara has 60 m of ribbon and she cuts 20 m ribbon that means 60 m – 20 m = 40 m.
So, length of ribbon will be left is 40 m.

16. (*a*) In the given picture, add all the weight that is 10 kg + 10 kg + 10 kg + 10 kg + 20 kg = 60 kg.
Therefore, the weight of the books are 60 kg.

17. (*b*) A scale measures in metre (m), a clock measures in second (s) and a thermometer measures in celsius (°C). So *A*, *B* and *C* are respectively metre (m), second (s) and celsius (°C).

Motion and Transport

1. (*d*) A girl is covering equal distance in equal interval of time shows uniform motion.
2. (*b*) Planets moving around the Sun is an example of circular motion.
3. (*c*) Water is the cheapest means of the transportation because it does not require expensive maintence as roads.
4. (*c*) Aeroplane is the fastest and bullock cart is the slowest means of transportation.
As, aeroplane needs a minutes to cover a distance of kilometre, while bullock cart takes an hour.
5. (*d*) Bullock cart and tonga are slow means of transport run by animals.
6. (*c*) Submarine is used by soldiers to travel under water, while sailboat, ship and boat are travel on water surface.
7. (*c*) Bullock cart, tonga, camel cart, cycle, all four vehicles have wheels in it. They are faster than the animals.
8. (*c*) Ship and motor boat both are mean of water transport.
9. (*b*) People used horses to travel in hilly areas. Camels are used to travel in deserts.
10. (*d*) Here, ship is the odd mean of transport. Other three modes of transport are airways. They are rocket, helicopter and air balloon.
11. (*c*) *X*-Aeroplane, *Y*-Boat.
12. (*c*) Land transport is not the most expensive mode of transportation. It is the safest mode of transportation.
13. (*c*) Rohan should avoid using water transport because it is the slowest mode of the transportation.
14. (*c*) A moving car's wheel, a rotating ceiling fan and a car travelling in circular path are examples of circular motion. However, a bouncing ball is an example of periodic motion.
15. (*c*) Bicycle is an environment friendly mode of transportation as it does not cause any pollution.
16. (*a*) Train, Bus, Cycle and Car all are mode of land transport.
17. (*b*) Ships are used to move huge amount of cargo. Ships are economically cheaper and can carry enormous weight.

Our Environment

1. (*d*) When water and wind can break rocks into small pieces, these small pieces convert into part of the soil.
2. (*d*) I. Throw garbage only at collection points.
II. Stop using plastic bags.
III. Water should be conserved.
3. (*a*) Noise that pollution - Unnecessary blowing horns
Air that pollution - Factory chimneys
Water pollution - Bathing in rivers with soap
Soil pollution - Use of plastics
4. (*a*) Humus, silt, clay and sand are all parts of soil.
5. (*b*) Wash floor daily with clean drinking water and burn fire crackers
These two activities we should not do to save water and make air fresh.
6. (*b*) Soil that cannot hold water - Sandy soil
Soil that is good for plant growth - Loamy soil
Soil particles are very fine - Clayey soil.
7. (*c*) We should use paper bags and we should give away old plastic toys to others who can use them.
8. (*b*) Air is invisible, it is essential for existence of life and moving air is called wind.
9. (*c*) Only statement in option (c) is correct, i.e. soil differ in size of particles and constituents.
10. (*b*) Air pollution around Taj Mahal area is discolouring its white colour. The cause of this air pollution is the release of harmful chemicals from the factories and vehicles into the air.
11. (*c*)

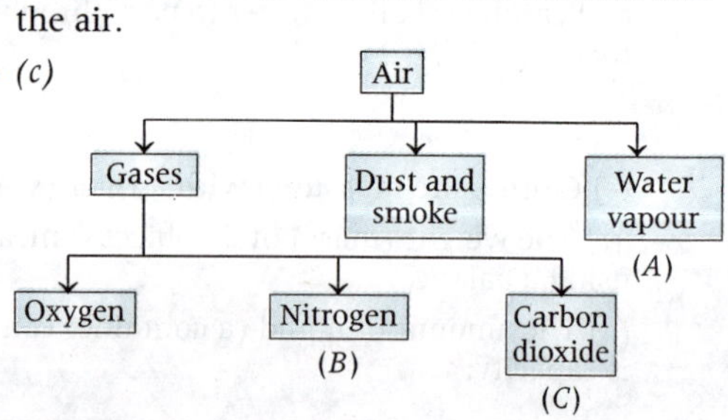

12. *(a)* In the given flow chart, soil is formed and it is the process of soil formation.
13. *(b)* Clayey soil is used by potter to make earthen pots as its has maximum water holding capacity.
14. *(c)* Both factories are responsible for water pollution. One is releasing toxic chemical and other release hot stream that harms the plants and aquatic animals.

Earth and Universe

1. *(a)* Earth is covered with 70% water, which gives it a blue colour, so it is also called the blue planet.
2. *(c)* The only planet with life in the solar system is Earth.
3. *(c)* The hottest planet of solar system is Venus.
4. *(b)* The Sun is heavenly body gives light to our solar system.
   Moon, Earth, Saturn, etc. do not have their own light.
5. *(d)* There is no air or water on the Moon. So, there are no plants or animals or people.
6. *(a)* The correct order of planets in our solar system is
   Mercury $\rightarrow$ Venus $\rightarrow$ Earth $\rightarrow$ Mars $\rightarrow$ Jupiter $\rightarrow$ Saturn $\rightarrow$ Uranus $\rightarrow$ Neptune
   Therefore, (a) is the correct option.
7. *(d)* According to the new definition of planet, Pluto is not a planet anymore. It is now called a dwarf planet.
8. *(b)* W is Sun, X is Earth and Y is Moon as Earth revolves around Sun and Moon revolves around Earth.
9. *(d)* The fixed path on which planet moves around the Sun is called orbit.
10. *(d)* The patterns formed by a group of stars in the sky is known as constellations.
11. *(c)* Option (c) is incorrect. The correct statement is 'An instrument known as **telescope** helps us to see the stars, the Moon and the planets clearly'.
12. *(a)* Earth is spherical in shape. It is made up of land, water and air. It rotates on its axis all the time and rotation causes day and night.
13. *(d)* Rotation is the phenomenon. The spinning movement of the Earth on its axis is called rotation.
14. *(a)* Both statements are true
    I. Stars have their own light.
    II. The Moon is the natural satellite of the Earth.
15. *(d)* The Sun is important for us as it gives us light to see things around and also it helps plants to make food. Sun does not give light to stars. They have their own light.
16. *(d)* **Jupiter** is the biggest planet of the solar system. **Saturn** is the planet with a system of the well-developed rings around it.
17. *(d)* The planet Moon have 3,475 km diameter and Earth has 12,756 km diameter and Sun have 1,391,016 km diameter. So, the order of increasing according to the sizes is,
    $$B \rightarrow A \rightarrow C.$$
18. *(c)* Earth rotates in its own axis. The Earth move around the Sun in a fixed path known as orbit and the Moon is the only natural satellite of the Earth. The Moon takes around $29\frac{1}{2}$ days to complete one revolution around the Earth.
19. *(b)* In the given flow chart P, Q and R are natural satellite, Moon and Earth respectively. Moon is the natural satellite of Earth, it takes $29\frac{1}{2}$ days to complete one revolution around the Earth.
    The Earth is only planet of our solar system where life exists.

Practice Set 1

1. *(b)*
2. *(a)*
3. *(a)*
4. *(c)*
5. *(a)* We should use Sun's energy whenever and wherever we can. This saves fuel and creates no pollution.
6. *(d)*
7. *(b)* When water vapour comes in contact with a cold plate, it cools down and turns back into drops of water.
8. *(d)* All the given birds have feathers covering their bodies.
9. *(c)* The change of water into water vapour on heating is called **evaporation**.
   The change of water vapour into water on cooling is called **condensation**.
10. *(b)* In the food pipe (B), digestion does not take place. Digestion takes place in mouth (chewing), stomach, and small intestine.
11. *(d)*
12. *(c)*
13. *(d)* Weather is a non-living (natural) thing.
14. *(c)* Flowers of plants produce seeds.

15. (*c*) Solar eclipse occurs when the Moon comes in between the Sun and the Earth.
16. (*c*) Human body consist of 206 bones.
17. (*c*) Sometimes, after it rains, a rainbow appears in the sky. It appears in the sky after rain when Sun rays strike with rain water.
18. (*a*) The standard unit for the measurement of time is second (s).
19. (*d*) Soil is made up of pieces of rocks, air, water and humus.
20. (*d*) Cow, dog and horse are domestic animals, whereas lion is a wild animal. Hence, lion is not domesticated by humans beings.
21. (*b*)
22. (*b*) The matter that has lot of free space between its particle is gas.
23. (*c*) Linear motion is a straight line motion.
24. (*c*) 25. (*c*) 26. (*b*)
27. (*a*) Lion is a wild animal and it stay in jungle hence, terrestrial. Lion eats flesh of other animals. Hence, it is carnivorous.
28. (*d*) Potato is a modified stem, whereas turnip, carrot and radish are modified roots.
29. (*b*) Pigeon can fly, penguin can swim but cannot fly and ostrich is a flightless bird and cannot swim also.
30. (*d*) Clayey soil is tightly packed with tiny grains.
31. (*d*) 32. (*d*)
33. (*d*) Throat has voice box that help us to speak.
34. (*c*) Humming birds have long and pointed beak to suck nectar from flowers.
35. (*d*)

Practice Set 2

1. (*b*) The movement of the Earth about its axis is called rotation. The rotation of the Earth is responsible for the formation of day and night.
2. (*c*) Leaves also have tiny pores called stomata on their lower surface. They helps in the exchange of gases.
3. (*c*) The skull protects the brain. The ribcage protect the heart and the lungs.
4. (*b*) Animals that eat both plants and flesh of other animals are called omnivores, e.g. mouse and pig.
Giraffe is herbivores and lion is carnivores.
5. (*a*) 6. (*b*)
7. (*c*) The Earth takes 365 days to complete one revolution, i.e. 365 days make one year. The revolution of the Earth around the Sun causes change in season.
8. (*a*) Liquids are measured in volume. $1\text{m}^3 = 1\text{L}$ (litre) 1 L signifies that his packet contains 1L juice.
9. (*d*) The circulatory system includes the heart, blood and blood vessels.
10. (*c*) *A* – Grasshopper, *B* – Snake
11. (*a*) Group *A*–Mammals, Group *B*–Birds Group *C*–Fishes.
12. (*b*)
13. (*b*) In ginger, the stem stores food and becomes swollen. The ginger we eat is actually a swollen stem.
14. (*a*)
15. (*b*) The movement of the Earth around the Sun in an orbit is called revolution.
16. (*d*) Plants produce oxygen, they remove carbon dioxide and contaminants from the air, they also provide habitat for birds and other wildlife.
17. (*d*) Rohan made an incorrect statement. Food protects us from illness and it helps us to fight against disease.
18. (*b*) Option (a), (c) and (d) are mode of air transport, but (b) is a water transport.
19. (*b*) Two major categories in which things can be classified are living and non-living things.
20. (*c*) The total distance travelled by girl is

$$\begin{aligned} &= 5\text{ km}\\ &= 10\text{ km}\\ &= 15\text{ km}\\ \hline &\ \ 30\text{ km} \end{aligned}$$

By adding all the distance, the total distance is 30 km.

21. (*b*) 22. (*c*) 23. (*d*)
24. (*c*) 25. (*c*) 26. (*c*)
27. (*c*) 28. (*b*) 29. (*c*)
30. (*d*) 31. (*b*) 32. (*b*)
33. (*d*)
34. (*c*) The length of the shadow of the given tree is double to their actual height. Hence, the actual length of tree *A* is 3 cm and the actual length of tree *B* is 14 cm.
35. (*b*)